ELVES AND FAIRIES

ELVES AND FAIRIES

A Short History of the Otherworld

MATTHIAS EGELER

TRANSLATED BY
STEWART SPENCER

YALE UNIVERSITY PRESS
NEW HAVEN AND LONDON

Elfen und Feen by Matthias Egeler originally published in German © Verlag C.H. Beck oHG, München 2024
Translation © 2025 by Stewart Spencer
First published in English by Yale University Press in 2025

All rights reserved. This book may not be reproduced in whole or in part, in any form (beyond that copying permitted by Sections 107 and 108 of the U.S. Copyright Law and except by reviewers for the public press) without written permission from the publishers.

All reasonable efforts have been made to provide accurate sources for all images that appear in this book. Any discrepancies or omissions will be rectified in future editions.

The publisher and author wish to thank the below for their permission to reproduce the following excerpts of texts.

J.R.R. Tolkien, *The Two Towers*, HarperCollins, London, 2011. Reprinted by permission of HarperCollins Publishers Ltd © 1954 J.R.R. Tolkien.
J.R.R. Tolkien, *On Fairy-stories*, HarperCollins, London, 2008. Reprinted by permission of HarperCollins Publishers Ltd © 1947 J.R.R. Tolkien.

For information about this and other Yale University Press publications, please contact:
U.S. Office: sales.press@yale.edu yalebooks.com
Europe Office: sales@yaleup.co.uk yalebooks.co.uk

Set in Adobe Garamond Pro by IDSUK (DataConnection) Ltd
Printed and bound in the UK using 100% renewable electricity at CPI Group (UK) Ltd

Library of Congress Control Number: 2025940610
A catalogue record for this book is available from the British Library.
Authorized Representative in the EU: Easy Access System Europe, Mustamäe tee 50, 10621 Tallinn, Estonia, gpsr.requests@easproject.com

ISBN 978-0-300-28440-9

10 9 8 7 6 5 4 3 2 1

For Odele

CONTENTS

Acknowledgements   ix

Introduction: Approaches to Elves and Fairies   1

Rural Elves and Fairies
1. Elves in Rural Iceland   13
2. Elves in Gaelic Ireland   41

Elves and Fairies at Court
3. From the Countryside to the Court: Fairies and Knights   73
4. From the Court to the Town: Between *A Midsummer Night's Dream*, Witchcraft and Learned Treatises   90

Urban Elves and Fairies
5. Between Scholarship, Poetry and Painting: The Urban Elves of the Nineteenth Century   113
6. A Change of Direction after the Turn of the Century: Elves and Fairies in the Early Twentieth Century, from Peter Pan to the Fairy Investigation Society   143
7. Elves and Fairies after the Second World War: International Popular Culture between Playing with History, Environmental Protection and the New Age   172

A Glance Backwards and into the Future
8   Coming Full Circle and the Taming of the Fairies   201

Endnotes   211
Further Reading   215
List of Illustrations and Maps   225
Index   227

ACKNOWLEDGEMENTS

This book could not have been written without the help of many people. I am especially grateful to the following: Michaela and Ulrich Berner; the Folklore Society; Julian Goodare; Wilhelm Heizmann; Jessica Hemming; Thomas Hessling; Carolyne Larrington; Caroline Oates; Johanna Schreiber; Jón Jónsson at the Research Centre of the University of Iceland in Strandir and, more especially, the local population of Strandir; Simon Young; and Odele Straub. The research that went into this little book was funded by the Deutsche Forschungsgemeinschaft (DFG), project numbers 317340660 and 453026744.

INTRODUCTION

Approaches to Elves and Fairies

In a remote mountain valley somewhere in Iceland, a small stream plunges over the Goðafoss Waterfall into a dark blue pool below. According to local legend, the owner of the farm there threw his statues of the ancient gods into the waterfall following Iceland's conversion to Christianity in the year 1000, hence its present name, Goðafoss, the 'Waterfall of the Gods'. A little further downstream is a geothermal field where the heat from Iceland's volcanic activity rises to just beneath the surface, creating a series of bubbling hot springs. In many geothermal fields in Iceland the result is a desert of boiling mud, but in the case of the field near Goðafoss, the visitor is greeted by the sight of a verdant meadow covered in a sea of brightly coloured flowers. The ground is so warm that it keeps the frost at bay and encourages the growth of very different and much richer flora than is to be found in the rest of the valley. Here the luxuriant vegetation covers an area of several hundred square metres. At its heart stand the grey and weathered ruins of a concrete

1. The ruins of the farmhouse near Goðafoss Waterfall that was built on a meadow belonging to the elves and destroyed by an avalanche.

structure, whose walls have shifted a good metre and a half away from its floor slab. A flourishing farmhouse once stood here. It was said that it had been built on lands where elves lived – land that should have remained inviolate – only the last farmer to live in this valley had refused to believe in such old wives' tales and had built a new home for himself on the very spot where the natural warmth of the earth would help to heat it during the long Icelandic winter. A few years later, the building was struck by an avalanche, dislodging it from its foundations and killing almost everyone inside. The elves' revenge was the death of an entire family (Illus. 1).

In another Icelandic valley a river plunges over a waterfall that is also called Goðafoss. This, too, is a 'Waterfall of the Gods', but it carries more water and is associated with a legend that plays a far more significant role in Icelandic history. This is the spot where the chieftain responsible for Iceland's abandonment of its pre-Christian gods and its acceptance of Christianity in the year 1000 threw his images of those gods into the waterfall. Here, too, there have been sightings of elves: the site now features a small service area with a souvenir shop overlooking the spectacular gorge where the river flows between sheer vertical walls of rock. If they are lucky, visitors will find whole armies of little elfin figures on display on the shelves. They have pointed ears and are holding flowers in their hands, while their caps are made of petals. These little flower fairies are now firmly established in Iceland, and anyone visiting the country today will find it hard to avoid them.

How do we get from the death-dealing elves at one Goðafoss to the cute little flower fairies that could almost be described as kitsch and that are sold to tourists at the other? Time and again we shall find variants of these two types of elf in present-day Iceland, whether on the signs beside hikers' trails, on maps, in the books of Icelandic seers and 'mediums' or in the historical archives. These two very different groups of elves coexist today, but between them lies a whole cultural history of their species. The present study sets out to tell their story.

In moving further and further apart, the two types of elf have followed the same lines of development as those that characterize the basic outlines of the cultural history of elves and fairies in Europe as a whole. Since Iceland has always been a part of Europe, an examination of the cultural history of elves and fairies in general may serve to explain the situation in Iceland in particular. This narrative begins and ends in Iceland, but if we are to understand how the vengeful elves in one of the two valleys became the flower fairies in the other, we need to trace the long lines of development that can be identified in the cultural history of elves and fairies in those places where these lines have unfolded and where fundamental changes can be seen to have taken place, namely, in Ireland, Scotland, England and, occasionally, in

Germany and North America. By their very nature, elves and fairies are international creatures.

Quite how international they are is pointedly illustrated by the example of German elves and fairies. The German words for elves and fairies are *Elfen* and *Feen*, and neither has a particularly long history: they both entered the language as loanwords in the eighteenth century, the first from English, the second from French. The German word *Fee* comes from the French *fée*, fairies being extremely popular in French fairytales (*contes de fées*). The German translators of these fairytales simply took over the French term *fée*. For its part, the German word *Elf* was borrowed from English, becoming part of the German language thanks to translations of works of English literature, most notably Shakespeare's *A Midsummer Night's Dream*. When the Brothers Grimm began work on their monumental German dictionary in the middle of the nineteenth century – at the time it was the most comprehensive work of modern lexicography of the German language – they initially baulked at this borrowing from another language and refused to include the word, preferring instead to establish the existence of an artificial word *Elb*, on the strength of medieval terms that by then had long since fallen into disuse. The third volume of their dictionary was published in 1862 and included the following entry:

> ELB, *m. genius . . . I have manufactured this word in order to replace the term* elf, *which is not a High German word at all and which had been thoughtlessly formed on the basis of the English word* elf *by speakers no longer mindful of their own term; in our own language* elf *sounds like someone mispronouncing the words* kalb *or* halb *as* kalf *or* half . . . *Without any further ado present-day writers use the forms* elfe *in the singular and* elfen *in the plural*.[1]

Despite the Grimms' squeamishness on this score, the English term has nonetheless prevailed, and their artificial construct of *Elben* is relatively rarely used – and often only when the text is intended to sound particularly archaic. In everyday conversation Germans use the English and French terms. What this means in the German-speaking world is that elves and fairies are not part of any ancient Germanic belief system, but may be described as an invasive species of supernatural beings, the result of an ongoing series of international exchange processes that have left a profound mark on the history of European cultures and religions. The history of cultures and of religions has always been a tale of contact and exchange, and this is no less true of elves and fairies than it is of other areas of our lives.

The cultural history of elves and fairies is an international phenomenon with a variety of offshoots and ramifications, repeatedly striking out in new directions and producing completely unexpected results, while other branches have vanished without trace. A short study like this one cannot explore all of these byways – for this an entire library would be necessary. As the literary scholar Diane Purkiss has noted, the population of the fairy realm has now grown too big to allow all of its inhabitants to be investigated in the space of a single volume.[2] And so the present study proposes no more than an initial introduction that provides a sketch of some of the more basic outlines of the cultural history of elves and fairies. A Further Reading section includes suggestions that will allow readers to explore the subject in greater depth.

The following chapters might be described as 'horseshoe-shaped', and attempt to present a compromise between a historical approach and a typological one. With regard to their overarching structure, they follow a sequence of historical developments, but at the same time, I have tried to bring out the types of elves and fairies that have emerged with particular clarity at certain times in our history and that continue to resonate in the cultural history of such creatures.

Our journey begins in traditional, rural Iceland, where elves or *álfar* have existed since the island was first settled in the ninth century. Iceland is believed to have been discovered in the years around 850, when the first settlers arrived. They came predominantly from Scandinavia, whose peoples expanded westwards in the early Middle Ages – during the time of the Vikings. This large-scale expansion had already led to an extensive acquisition of land in Scotland and Ireland, with the result that many of the earliest settlers who came to Iceland arrived not direct from Scandinavia, but from Gaelic-speaking Scotland and Ireland. This meant that from the very outset, Icelandic culture had a pronounced Gaelic element to it – an element that has also left its mark on the cultural history of elves and fairies: several Icelandic legends about elves and many aspects of the traditional, popular belief in elves were influenced by Gaelic culture. After examining rural Iceland, I shall turn, therefore, to medieval Ireland and Scotland and to the traditional folk beliefs held in those regions. After all, it is to Ireland and Scotland that we can trace the origins of many of the ideas that have left such a lasting mark on traditional views of elves and fairies in Iceland.

After presenting an outline of the Gaelic traditions that relate to elves, in the following chapters my emphasis remains on the British Isles and its surrounding areas, where some of the greatest changes in terms of the evolution of elves and fairies took place. Among the milestones in this development are the medieval narratives about King Arthur and his knights of the Round Table (together with the echo of these tales in later Scottish ballads) and developments in England during the early modern period, when Shakespeare's *A Midsummer Night's Dream* proved one of the most influential works on the subject of elves and fairies. It was also at around this time that elves and fairies were first mentioned in Scottish witch trials, often featuring as important elements in the indictment, many Scottish witches (and sorcerers) allegedly having consorted directly with these creatures.

This Scottish belief in an intercourse between fairies and witches brings us to the seventeenth century and even slightly later. By the end of the eighteenth century we start to find a number of other important innovations among English artists and writers. Only now did fairies sprout wings. Only now did the Brothers Grimm establish folklore as a subject for serious scholarly enquiry – research that was quickly taken up in the English-speaking world and that introduced the traditions of the 'simple folk' to middle-class artists active in the towns and cities. In turn, this led to a flourishing interest in elves and fairies on the part of artists and literary figures, in the process laying the foundations for their present-day popularity.

The early twentieth century witnessed a number of key events, including the affair of the Cottingley fairies, a series of photographs that gave another important impetus to the idea of elves and fairies that continues to be felt today. Those who held older and, more especially, traditionally rural views about elves and fairies conceived of them as powerful, often dangerous, and at the very least ambivalent creatures, but from the time of the Cottingley fairies, if not before, this view faded in significance, to be replaced by a perception of elves and fairies as cute little creatures associated with flowers and petals. In turn, this development facilitated a change of attitude from traditional elves and fairies who could wipe out an entire family in an act of revenge to the plastic figurines of little flower fairies.

But this period also saw a countermovement, especially after the Second World War, when J.R.R. Tolkien returned to the medieval sources and created his own brand of elf, emphatically rejecting the figure of the flower fairy. As a result, I have devoted the final chapter before the Conclusion to the evolution of elves and fairies in twentieth- and twenty-first-century literature. We shall then make our way back to Iceland, at which point I shall describe how international developments have affected present-day perceptions of elves and fairies there. During the twentieth century, the elves and fairies of the British Isles came to exert a powerful influence on those of Iceland for a second time. During the Viking Age, the traditional elves of the Gaelic world helped to mould their Icelandic counterparts, and today the Icelandic elves that were formed under Gaelic influence have again been reshaped by the elves and fairies that have evolved in the British Isles over the last millennium. This second, modern reshaping of Iceland's elves brings us to the fairies of the self-proclaimed seer and 'Elves' Representative' Erla Stefánsdóttir, with whom we end.

While tracing this horseshoe-shaped trajectory from Iceland to Ireland and Great Britain, and from there back to Iceland, I also take a different journey: from the countryside to the towns. The cultural history of elves and fairies is a story of cultural contact and of international cultural transfer. Additionally, however, it is the story of a reinterpretation of traditional beliefs that had originated among the rural population by an urban audience that sought to adapt rural ideas to suit very different circumstances, including their own problems and interests. In this process, the courtly literature of the Middle Ages played an important role as a stepping stone and as an intermediary stage. As a result, it is possible to describe the tale of elves and fairies as the story of the relocation of rural legends to aristocratic courts, and from there to towns and cities and a middle-class milieu. There are multiple exceptions to this rule, of course; and by and large, complex melanges are more common than simple, linear developments. But as a general trend, the movement from rural areas to towns provides a useful basic template in tracing the evolution of elves and fairies.

I should like to end this Introduction with a brief word about the object of this book. The following chapters provide the reader with a cultural history of a group of creatures traditionally described in their countries of origin with the Romance word *fée* and the Germanic word 'elf'. (I am using the term 'Germanic' here in its historical linguistic sense.) In modern German and modern English, the words *Fee*/*fairy* (both of which are ultimately French in origin) and *Elf*/*elf* are largely synonymous – even if, more recently, there has been a discernible tendency to think of fairies as small and winged, whereas Tolkien's heroic elves are human in stature. As a Celtic language, Irish uses different terms, but in Anglo-Irish the word *fairies* is used in an entirely self-evident way to describe the figures of the autochthonous Gaelic tradition. The Icelandic word *álfur*, meaning 'elf', is part of the same linguistic complex, since it is cognate with – and the linguistic equivalent of – the English word *elf* and the German word *Elf*. Icelandic, English and German are all members of the same Germanic family of languages, and in this case they all use what in terms of historical linguistics is one and the same word.

This study examines fairies and elves in the narrower sense, to the extent that the creatures that form the object of my enquiry are described by exactly these words – or by their linguistic equivalents – in the countries that are their homes. On the other hand, this book is not a general history of nature spirits. Such a history would take us off in very different directions – and much further afield – even if elves and fairies have, at a certain point in their history, been reinterpreted as nature spirits. This is only one aspect of the story of elves and fairies, just as – conversely – elves and fairies are only one aspect of a general history of nature spirits.

In tracing the history of elves and fairies, this study avails itself of what, from a historical standpoint, is the prevailing linguistic usage. Although the terms 'fairies' and 'elves' derive from two different linguistic families – the Romance and the Germanic – they largely overlap in terms of their use. Only in specific contexts have different semantic nuances evolved. In general, the two terms are interchangeable and will be used in this way in the course of the following chapters. If there are historical differences on points of individual detail, I shall follow the historical usage that is relevant to the specific instances, as should be clear from the particular context.

Rural Elves and Fairies

CHAPTER 1

ELVES IN RURAL ICELAND

Whenever native German speakers use the words 'Iceland' and 'elves' in the same sentence, listeners will automatically expect a further catchword to follow – namely, *Elfenbeauftragte*, which could be translated as the 'Elves' Representative'. Many Germans to this day believe that Iceland has a state-appointed 'Elves' Representative', though the name of the woman who first gave rise to the idea that such an office exists – the Icelandic theosophist Erla Stefánsdóttir (1935–2015) – is scarcely known. Nevertheless, she has played a prominent role in the Germans' perception of Iceland, and continues to do so, more especially in terms of tourism; the 'elf maps' that she produced are still sold throughout the Reykjavík area.

Our picture of elves has changed over time, and varies according to the social and geographical context. In Iceland, we need to draw a clear and fundamental distinction between three such contexts, each of which has its own particular view of elves: medieval Iceland, which was predominantly rural in character, with no conurbations, but whose political and social elites nonetheless produced an extensive body of scholarly writing; the modern transmission of folktales from Iceland's rural areas; and the modern urban areas, chief of which is the Reykjavík region. Erla Stefánsdóttir's fairies belong to the third of these contexts – Iceland's urban areas – and are closely associated with the little plastic figures of flower fairies on sale in Iceland's souvenir shops. The greater part of this book will be given over to an explanation of the way in which this kind of elf evolved and how it came to Iceland, and so I shall not return to Erla Stefánsdóttir until Chapter 7. Our story of elves and fairies, conversely, begins in the countryside in the Middle Ages. Over the course of the following chapters we shall trace their journey, step by step, from the countryside to the modern conurbation.

Iceland in the Middle Ages: The *álfar*

Medieval Iceland produced one of the most extensive vernacular literatures in the whole of Europe, a literature that, in turn, gave rise to a vast variety of sagas, poems, historical treatises and religious and legal texts. Despite the richness of this literature, elves are rarely mentioned here – and then the allusions to them are often extremely vague.

Our knowledge of elves in medieval Iceland begins with their name. In Old Norse literature – in other words, the literature of medieval Iceland and Scandinavia – the term *álfr* (plural *álfar*) is used to describe a particular group of supernatural beings. It is generally assumed by present-day scholars that the word *álfr* derives from an older Indo-European word, **albh-*, meaning 'white' or 'bright'. This term has precise counterparts in other languages that make up the Germanic family of languages. In terms of historical linguistics, *álfr* is cognate with Old English *ælf* and Old High German *alp*, a word that has survived in modern German as the first element in the word *Alptraum*, meaning 'nightmare'. But in medieval Iceland the word *álfr* was far from having the same sort of negative connotations as we might assume from the term *Alptraum* ('nightmare'). In two of the poems that are included in the Poetic, or Elder, Edda the word *álfrǫðull*, meaning 'elfin beam', is a poetic synonym for the sun, which suggests that at this period elves were associated with light and with brightness.

Hardly any proper names of elves have come down to us from the Norse Middle Ages, when they were mostly referred to as a collective. But the way in which this collective appears in Old Norse poetry generally implies that elves were seen in a positive light. In skaldic verse – a type of poetry composed to honour Norse heroes and their deeds – elves are regularly mentioned in poetic circumlocutions to refer to glorious warriors, which once again implies a positive association with the contemporary ideal of manhood. At the same time, these poems include no equivalent comparison between elves and women: whenever the skaldic poets wanted to describe a woman whom they deemed worthy of their praise, they would refer to a supernatural being from the class of *dísir*. In the oldest layer of our surviving sources, elves/*álfar* appear to have been the masculine counterpart to the feminine *dísir*. Not until later, during the High Middle Ages, do we encounter unequivocal evidence of female *álfar*, perhaps because the clear-cut distinction between *álfar* and *dísir* had already been abandoned by this date.

Elves also have positive connotations in the mythological poems of the Elder Edda, a collection of poems about gods and heroes that has come down to us primarily in a manuscript compiled in the thirteenth century and today known as the Codex Regius. Scholars now include a number of other thematically related poems within this corpus of works. Several of these poems use the fixed poetic formula *ása oc álfa* – 'of Æsir and of elves' – to describe the supernatural forces that control the world, in that way placing elves in close proximity to the gods.

In a handful of texts, the *álfar* even appear to be equated with one of the two families of Old Norse gods. Medieval Icelandic literature divides the gods into two groups: the Æsir and the Vanir. In some of these texts the term *álfar* is used to refer to the Vanir, a point that emerges with particular clarity from *Lokasenna* (*Loki's Quarrel*), one of the mythological poems from the Poetic Edda. In these texts, the *álfar* are not only said to be close to the gods, but even appear to be a subgroup of them. That there is a close connection between the world of the gods and that of the elves is clear from a line in the *Grímnismál* (*The Sayings of Grímnir*), according to which the god Freyr, who is one of the Vanir, received Álfheimr – the 'Home of the Elves' – as a gift.

But the picture that these Old Norse texts have to offer us is by no means a uniform one. Other mythological poems draw a clear distinction between the Æsir, the Vanir and the *álfar*. The poem *Alvíssmál* (*The Sayings of All-Wise*), for example, describes the various languages spoken by the Æsir, Vanir, elves, dwarves, giants and humans, suggesting that there is a difference between these categories of being. It is also worth mentioning in passing that this poem was almost certainly the source of inspiration for the languages spoken by the Elves, Dwarves and Men in Tolkien's *The Lord of the Rings*. In short, the sources do not provide us with a unified picture. This lack of clarity is especially striking in the handful of material that has come down to us relating to individual names in these groups of supernatural beings. Take the name Gandálfr. It means 'the elf who can do magic' and appears to be the name of an elf. It also inspired Tolkien with the name of his sorcerer, Gandalf. But in Old Norse literature it appears in a list of the names of dwarves, a list that also includes Vindálfr ('Wind Elf'). In short, the boundaries between elves and dwarves appear to have been just as indistinct as those between elves and gods.

Only a single detailed account of a named *álfr* has come down to us from Old Norse literature: another of the poems that make up the Poetic Edda, the *Vǫlundarkviða* (*The Lay of Vǫlundr*), tells the story of Vǫlundr the smith, better known in Germany as Wieland and in the English-speaking world as Wayland. Vǫlundr is one of the *álfar* and is an incomparable craftsman, whose skills as a smith are unmatched. He almost certainly inspired the elfin smiths in *The Lord of the Rings*, where the elves are likewise known for their metalwork skills. The first part of this Old Norse poem tells how Vǫlundr becomes amorously involved with a woman from the otherworld. Once this woman has left him, he remains at home, fashioning trinkets that he hopes to give her on her return. But his accomplishments as a smith attract the greed of others, and a king by the name of Niðuðr takes him prisoner and severs the sinews on his knees, leaving him lame. Niðuðr then forces Vǫlundr to work for him. But in the process, the king brings misfortune down on his family. Vǫlundr waits for the right moment, and when his chance comes, he kills the king's two sons, before encasing their skulls in silver and reworking their eyes and teeth as jewels. He then gets Niðuðr's daughter drunk and makes her pregnant, before rising up into the air (it is not entirely clear from the poem how he manages to do this) and shouting down to the ground to tell Niðuðr all the details of the revenge he has wreaked on the king and his family. He then flies away, leaving Niðuðr in his palace, a broken man.

This poem contains many passages – including ones that identify Vǫlundr as an *álfr* – that are hard to interpret both linguistically and in terms of their content. One of the questions that the poem raises but fails to answer is how the cruelty of Vǫlundr's vengeance can be reconciled with the predominantly positive picture of *álfar* in Old Norse literature. Writers have foisted many a conflicting reading on this problematical poem. One such attempt at an interpretation argues that Vǫlundr's behaviour remains within the framework of that shown by other, 'positive' figures in Old Norse literature, inasmuch as he is not guilty of any unprovoked aggression. Vǫlundr is merely reacting to the wrongs that he has suffered, and if vengeance strikes the innocent, rather than the truly guilty, and if it is disproportionate in its severity, then this is by no means unusual within the context of Old Norse narrative culture. As a tale about an *álfr*, the poem depicts Vǫlundr as a gifted smith who is not intrinsically evil, but whose vengeance assumes the most terrible form imaginable. This idea of the *álfar* exacting revenge is a motif that continues to resonate in the tales of present-day Iceland, as well as in others from the fairly recent past. The flattened farmstead near the Goðafoss Waterfall is by no means the only example, which we shall be returning to in due course.

There are very few signs that elves were worshipped – and even where they exist, the details are unreliable. The oldest and most important evidence takes the form of the *Austrfararvísur* (*Strophes on the Journey to the East*), which probably dates from the late Viking Age, in other words the eleventh century. Here the skald Sigvatr Þórðarson describes a journey that he took to Sweden in 1018 at the behest of the king of Norway. This was at a time when Iceland was undergoing a major change from a pre-Christian to a Christian culture. In the course of his poem, Sigvatr adopts a tone that leaves a distinctly comic impression as he describes the struggles that he has been forced to endure. One of the challenges that he claims to have had to face was the unfriendliness of the local population. His travelogue tells how, foot-sore and weary from his journey, he finds himself standing outside a farmstead, where he fails to find the hospitable welcome that he had expected. Instead, he is turned away by the woman who opens the door, since the people who live here are pagans and are currently celebrating an *álfablót* or 'elf sacrifice'. In his account, Sigvatr goes on to recall how he was similarly and unceremoniously turned away from each of the next three farms.

As a poem, the *Strophes on the Journey to the East* is important as the oldest surviving evidence that elves may have been an object of cultic veneration. According to these lines, this cult was a matter for individual farmsteads, although it remains unclear to what extent Sigvatr's account is based on true events and on his own experience. First and foremost, the poem is a satire written by a Norwegian Christian keen to depict the Swedes as pagan backwoodsmen lacking both manners and the true faith. It is no longer possible to say with any certainty whether the sacrifice that Sigvatr describes as being offered up to the elves was real, or whether he invented it in order to make fun of the Swedes in the eyes of his audience. Apart from the *Strophes on the Journey to the East*, there are only two other Old Norse texts that mention sacrifices offered up to elves. Both of them date from the thirteenth century and describe acts of worship in pre-Christian Iceland, as seen from the standpoint of several centuries later. It is possible that the *álfar* were once the object of cultic veneration, but this is by no means certain.

In short, much of what we know about the *álfar* on the basis of Old Norse texts is either vague or ambiguous, and certainly does not amount to a uniform picture. One of the reasons for this may be the differences in Nordic perceptions of the *álfar* that varied depending on the time and the place. The evidence that I have already considered comes from a vast geographical area extending from Sweden to Iceland. More recent research on the history of Old Norse religion has shown that we are dealing with a considerable degree of local variations within the area, and the *álfar* can have been no exception. Our sources, moreover, cover a period of three centuries – from the end of the Viking Age in the tenth and eleventh centuries to High Medieval literature of the thirteenth. We can assume that over this time there were far-reaching changes in contemporaries' ideas about the *álfar*, even if those changes can no longer be reconstructed in any great detail.

But there is at least one important source in which we can observe innovatory forces at work. From around 1220, the Icelandic politician and scholar Snorri Sturluson (1178/79–1241) began to compile a kind of handbook of Old Norse poetry: the Snorra Edda, also known as the Prose Edda (Illus. 2). Norse poetry regularly uses mythological allusions to make its point, and, as we have already noted, the *álfar* are often found in poetic paraphrases for warriors. The role of mythology in poetry meant that Snorri's handbook devotes a good deal of space to an account of Norse mythology. In an overview of the principal places in the cosmos, he writes of the *álfar*:

> Many splendid places are there. There is one place that is called Alfheim. There live the folk called light-elves [*ljósálfar*], but dark-elves [*døkkálfar*] live down in the ground, and they are unlike them in appearance, and even more unlike them in nature. Light-elves are fairer than the sun to look at, but dark-elves are blacker than pitch.[1]

2. An eighteenth-century Icelandic manuscript of the Snorra Edda.

Snorri goes on to state that there are three heavens, one on top of the other, and that the light-elves are at present the only beings that inhabit the highest of them.

The importance of this passage lies not in what it tells us about elves, but in the unusual clarity with which a medieval mythographer can be seen at work here. Snorri is not content with merely writing down traditional material: he also attempts to impose some order on it and to systematize it. And here he takes his cue from what was known about the organization of the cosmos at this time, an understanding influenced in turn by Christian theology. One of the most influential theological works of this period was the *Elucidarius* – a Latin text, but one that existed in an Old Norse translation. Here it is said that the cosmos is structured in such a way that it is in the highest of the three heavens that the angels can glimpse God. This treatise also mentions another detail: namely, that the angels are 'seven times fairer than the sun', which is exactly what Snorri writes about the light-elves. Like the angels in the *Elucidarius*, they live in the highest of the three heavens and are fairer than the sun. In this case, we can not only say in the most general terms that Snorri's contrast between light-elves and dark-elves takes as its starting point the Christian distinction between angels and fallen angels (or demons) and projects it on to the *álfar*, but we can even say exactly which theological source he used.

The two terms *ljósálfar* (light-elves) and *døkkálfar* (dark-elves) were neologisms coined by Snorri and are found nowhere else in Old Norse literature, which means in turn that his account contains very little traditional material. It does, however, provide us with important evidence of the way in which a scholarly writer of the thirteenth century perceived the *álfar*: namely, as figures that may have been ambivalent, but that in many respects could be placed in parallel with the angels of Christian theology. What we can see here, in short, is an early attempt to integrate the *álfar* into the Christian cosmos. By the nineteenth century, this process was almost complete; and yet it was a very different strategy from the one adopted by Snorri that ultimately prevailed.

The Narrated Landscape in Modern Iceland: The Hidden People

Our medieval accounts of elves are taken from the writings of a social elite: although many of the poems of the period were orally transmitted, it was only when they were written down that the tradition achieved any permanence. At least to the extent that we are able to say this today, writers such as Snorri Sturluson worked for the most part within a framework marked by the written word. Within this context, other textual sources were similarly reworked. A particularly good example of this is Snorri's use of the *Elucidarius*: in order to elaborate his own (written) account of the *álfar*, he fell back on some of the scholarly material that was available to him in written form. In this case, it was an Old Norse translation of a theological treatise in Latin. It is important to stress this emphasis on the written word, since it involves a key proviso: nothing that has come down to us from the Middle Ages could be described as the ideas of the 'common people'. What has reached us are literary – and in some cases fictional – constructs on the part of a highly educated upper echelon of society. These sources have nothing to do with popular belief, but are scholarly in origin.

If, on the other hand, we turn our attention to the Iceland of the more recent past, we find that the situation is fundamentally different. In the early nineteenth century, the Brothers Grimm emerged as the founding fathers of the scientific study of folklore. Thanks to their extensive activities in collecting, publishing and analysing myths and legends, they created in large sections of the educated population an awareness of the cultural value of the oral tradition in rural communities – communities previously largely ignored by writers from the upper classes. (I shall have more to say on this subject in Chapter 5.) This new fascination with folktales and fairy stories soon reached Iceland, too, where it led to the first systematic collections of autochthonous narratives. In turn, this bout of activity among collectors very quickly revealed the wealth of the oral tradition in rural communities,

Jón Árnason alone documenting around 2,600 fairytales, folktales and legends in the middle of the nineteenth century, while the research that has been conducted since then has demonstrated the extent to which this was merely the tip of the iceberg.

Clear differences exist between the elves described by the literary culture of the upper strata of medieval society and those in the largely oral rural culture of the nineteenth and twentieth centuries. These differences begin with the terminology that they use. In medieval literary texts, the predominant term is *álfar* (elves), which is, in fact, the only word that is documented as being used until the thirteenth century. Not until the fourteenth century do we find the first scattered evidence for the use of the term *huldumaður*, meaning 'hidden human being'. And not until the nineteenth and twentieth centuries is the term *huldufólk* (Hidden People) found as a common alternative to *álfar* in the language of rural communities.

In rural Iceland, the Hidden People are no longer found in the world of heroic legend, as was the case with the medieval *Lay of Vǫlundr*, or in the sort of poetological and cosmological speculations that we associate with Snorri Sturluson, but in the everyday world of agricultural labour. The Hidden People of today are best described as a parallel society of farmers dwelling in rocks and hills in the immediate vicinity of human farmhouses. Today's elves are no longer thought of primarily as men, as appears to have been the case with the earliest medieval evidence, but are part of a society of men and women; meanwhile there is at least regional evidence to suggest that, in modern tales about elves, it is the women of the Hidden People who play the more dominant role, while their male counterparts tend to retreat into the background. 'Hidden People' is a term that covers the whole range of a fully functioning rural world: in addition to men and women, local legends also mention the children, cattle and even the trading posts of the Hidden People, whose lives are therefore a mirror image of human life. And like the members of human society, the Hidden People are livestock farmers raising sheep, goats and cows. The stories associated with them tell of encounters with their 'hidden cattle' just as they tell of encounters with the Hidden People themselves. In terms of their religion, too, the Hidden People are a mirror image of the human society found in Iceland, a country that by tradition is Protestant – and more specifically Lutheran. The Hidden People of present-day Iceland hold Christian beliefs, and even have their own clergy and their own churches. Even Snorri had tried to place elves in a Christian cosmos, but where he equated them with angels, more recent folktales achieve this integration by describing the elves as a parallel society of good and God-fearing Christians.

In popular legend, the Hidden People do not live in Heaven, as they did with Snorri, but – significantly – in the immediate proximity of human beings. In the world of traditional storytelling in rural Iceland, the hills and rocks associated with elves are among the most frequent settings for supernatural narratives. These elfin dwellings are identified with very specific, readily perceptible places in the local countryside, and in most cases they have specific, recurring features. The Hidden People typically live in free-standing rocks or in hills, the size of which can be measured in human terms – somewhere between a summerhouse and a two-bedroom house. The members of the Hidden People are the same size as ordinary humans, and their dwellings, too, are mostly comparable in scale. There are, of course, exceptions; but in general, neither small stones nor cliffs several hundred metres high are associated with elves. On at least one of its sides, a hillock typically associated with elves has a rocky face that may reflect the wood-panelled façade found on traditional farmhouses in nineteenth-century Iceland. The homes of the Hidden People are, for the most part, located in places that follow a largely fixed pattern: in general, the hills and rocks associated with elves are near the heart of an Icelandic farmstead and lie in the immediate vicinity of the main building, not more than a few minutes' walk away and often clearly visible from the farmhouse. Not infrequently, these elves are a farmer's closest neighbours.

There are times when it is difficult to distinguish between the Hidden People and ordinary human beings. According to the local folktales that circulated in rural Iceland in the nineteenth and early twentieth centuries, the Hidden People are in almost every case the same size as humans. Physically, they look just like human beings, and they dress in exactly the same way. It is important to stress that point, because this characteristic has undergone a rapid and dramatic change in the urban setting of present-day Reykjavík. We shall later examine this change in greater detail, but for now it is enough to note that within an urban context there has been an increasing tendency for the traditional elves that were barely distinguishable from human beings to become aligned and equated with the small and often winged creatures of popular Anglophone culture. In short, the 'Reykjavík fairy' and the Hidden People traditionally found in rural areas have evolved in radically different directions. In traditional rural narratives, the only recurrent difference between humans and elves is that the Hidden People may wear more colourful clothes than their human neighbours.

The bright colours of elves' clothing have a social connotation. In the context of the poverty that was widespread in nineteenth-century Iceland, the luxury of colourful clothes was an indication of the sort of wealth that many people could only dream about. The relative affluence of elfin society implies that this parallel society reflects not reality, but the desires and aspirations of human society. At the same time, however, the gulf between human society and that of the Hidden People is never particularly large: after all, some stories also tell of the poverty of individual families of elves, who have to borrow food from human farmers in order to get by.

The world of humans is so tightly interwoven with the world of the Hidden People that the two of them repeatedly come into contact with each other. One of the themes frequently found in tales of the Hidden People is of the encounters that take place on the open road. Time and again, we find examples of someone going from A to B and meeting some strangers, and since it subsequently turns out that no one can identify these strangers, it is concluded – in the absence of any other explanation – that they were members of the Hidden People. According to a nineteenth-century account, one such incident is said to have taken place on the road between the Kaldbakur and Kleifar farms in the Bay of Kaldbaksvík, where, one moonlit winter's night, two travellers met a group of four or five people dressed in blue. They were heading in the opposite direction and were not known to either of the travellers. It was no more than a brief encounter, and no words were exchanged, but the two travellers were puzzled as to the strangers' identities. They made enquiries and, when those enquiries proved fruitless, they began to suspect that the strangers had been members of the Hidden People. The story stresses the plausibility of this interpretation of events by mentioning the colour of the strangers' clothing: by moonlight, the colour blue is almost impossible to identify; and yet it is very much the colour that is emphasized in this account, more especially because blue (or red) is typical of the more expensive clothing worn by the Hidden People.

In Iceland, in traditional rural life there is a common type of supernatural place that often indicates (albeit indirectly) the presence of the Hidden People: the *álagablettur*. This term simply means a 'place of enchantment', yet the enchantment associated with these places is always a very specific one. An *álagablettur* is a piece of land – most often a meadow or a rock formation – that is not used by humans (or if it is, then such use is strictly regulated). In most cases it is a small stretch of grassland where the grass cannot be cut, but these places are also frequently hills where it is forbidden to mow the grass or to quarry rocks. If these rules are broken, the infringement is immediately punished – typically with the death of an animal, such as a cow that has eaten the grass at an *álagablettur*; or someone may be seriously injured by the blade of a scythe while mowing the grass.

In the majority of cases, however, there are no detailed stories associated with these 'magic places', which are merely designated as such: people are told that if they damage the place, they will be punished. If detailed stories are told at all, they mostly follow the pattern of 'ban – infringement – punishment – change of heart': people are banned from encroaching on the magic place; the ban is ignored; the guilty parties are punished; and, having learnt their lesson, they leave the magic place inviolate in the future. To take an example: a section of the embankment of the River Víðidalsá in Iceland's Westfjords region is called Huldufólksbrekka (Hidden People's River Bank) and the locals report that this river bank is one of these magic places. When, in the second half of the twentieth century, a new farmer took over the property on this site, he was told that he must leave Huldufólksbrekka alone, but the farmer thought this was a foolish superstition and allowed his favourite horse to graze there. Retribution followed as night follows day: the horse fell down the river bank, broke its back and died.

Few stories about these magic places give an explicit reason for the ban on the use of the land in question. Huldufólksbrekka is an example of the way in which these bans are explained in those cases in which an explanation is offered at all. After all, the very name means 'Hidden People's River Bank', and already in the 1940s, the owner of the farm told a collector of folktales that people were banned from violating the river bank because it belonged to the Hidden People.

The punishment that follows the infringement of such a ban may assume the most drastic proportions, but it does not necessarily have to do so. It is said that in the middle of the twentieth century a farmer cut the grass in a forbidden area of his farm in the fjord Ingólfsfjörður in the Westfjords region. The following night the farmer's wife saw an elfin woman in a dream. The elf explained that she needed the grass to feed her two goats during the winter. In order to make good the harm they had done, the farmer and his wife were required to take over this responsibility, with the result that throughout the following winter they set aside a corner of their indoor sheepfold big enough for two goats. The sheep never went into that corner and all the hay that the farmer threw into it disappeared. In this way, the incident ended on a note of reconciliation. But similar tales were told about other farms where violating a place reserved for the Hidden People led to manifestly more serious consequences. I have already referred to one such example in the Introduction: the destruction of the farm at Goðafoss Waterfall, where the farmer's encroachment on a prohibited area led to the destruction of the farm in an avalanche during the winter of 1948/49 and to the death of almost all the farmer's family. This disaster – and its ostensibly supernatural causes – hit the headlines in the Icelandic press at the time. A headline in the newspaper *Vísir* read:

> TRAGEDY IN GOÐDALUR: HE STARTED AN ARGUMENT WITH AN ENCHANTMENT – AND NOW THE FARMSTEAD LIES IN RUINS.

In its sensationalist way, this headline makes clear the extent of the threat that local legends – and national newspapers – can impute to this act of infringement. Despite the fact that they are associated with death and disaster, these magic places – alleged to belong to the Hidden People – remain the most widespread type of supernatural site in Iceland. In those places where there is evidence from the nineteenth and early twentieth century to document the association between old farmsteads and stories about the Hidden People, the existence of these places is attested to with such frequency that we can assume that before the Second World War each farm had at least one site on its property that humans were forbidden to violate.

In the light of these traditions, one of the big questions facing researchers working in the field of religious beliefs is why the idea of these forbidden places was manifestly so attractive. If this type of place was so dangerous that there was the permanent risk of the farm's destruction, why was one (or more) such site identified on almost every farm? The local folktales offer no explanation for this, but simply accept the existence of these places as a given. Yet anyone looking at this tradition from the outside is bound to ask the question 'Why?'

It is impossible to provide an unequivocal answer to this, although we may surmise that one factor is the power that these places had with regard to accidents: the forbidden places of the Hidden People determine if and when misfortune strikes. The relevant tales tend above all to describe the way in which the violation of such a place brings with it misfortune, and yet the power of these places seems also to have suggested that the argument be turned on its head: all that one has to do to avert disaster is to avoid the place. Within the surviving corpus of Icelandic tales there are indeed isolated examples of the idea that if the place in question is respected, its supernatural owner will reward this act of kindness by preventing any mishap from befalling not only the place itself, but also the surrounding area. Work on a farm is always dangerous and subject to all manner of vagaries: workplace accidents, bad weather and livestock diseases are constant and uncontrollable risks. In unpredictable times, a forbidden place may have conveyed a feeling of certainty and security by prescribing clear and simple rules which, if followed, would avert disaster. This way of thinking helped landowners deal emotionally with the imponderables of their precarious lives. It was a kind of emotional insurance that involved the farmer in little extra expense, since the places concerned were typically very small.

The forbidden places of the Hidden People illustrate the ambivalence of the relationship between human beings and their supernatural neighbours: relations between humans and elves on a farm may be good or bad, and a farmer's dealings with the Hidden People and the places associated with them may have consequences that likewise may be good or bad. This ambivalence is a recurring theme in traditional Icelandic narratives about the Hidden People – a theme that permeates every kind of folktale on the subject of elves and fairies.

Another widespread theme in these tales is the motif of an amorous affair between a human and an elf. In some cases a human male is involved with an elfin female; in other cases the relationship is reversed. The majority of these tales describe the relationship as a source of unbounded joy. A farmer at the Steingrímsfjord in the eighteenth century is said to have had an affair with an elf widow who lived in the boulder Ekkjusteinn (Widow Stone) on his land, and that their actions had no negative consequences. Yet counterexamples exist likewise: of another farmer in the same fjord it was said that he had had an affair with a female elf who lived in the rocks on his property, but that he then had to move away, causing him to feel depressed for the rest of his life.

Elves can also help humans – and sometimes in a very basic way. It is said of the now abandoned farm at Þiðriksvellir, in a mountain valley above the Steingrímsfjord, that a shepherd was driven to such distraction by his sheep that he turned for help to a female elf who lived in the Stúlkuhóll (Girl's Hill) close to the farm and dedicated a poem to her:

Faldaskorðin farðu á ról	Good lady, get a move on.
fremd þín ekki dvínar;	Your honour will not fade.
stúlkan góða í Stúlkuhól	Good girl in Girl's Hill,
stöðvaðu kindur mínar.	stop my beasts from roaming.[2]

He then had no more problems with his sheep in the vicinity of Girl's Hill.

On the other hand, the Hidden People are portrayed in an entirely negative light in tales of *umskiptingar*, or changelings. These tales describe how human children are stolen by elves and replaced by the children of the Hidden People. They also explain the precautions that humans can take to prevent their children from being taken from them, and the ways in which they can win those children back. Even very simple measures can provide a degree of assurance – by adding a cross to the cradle, for example, since elves cannot steal a child from a cradle that has been blessed in this way. If, despite such measures, elves still succeed in spiriting a child away from its parents, it helps to beat or mistreat the changeling, as the elves will then reclaim their own child. Of course, the parents must then endure the reproaches of the elves for having mistreated their infant, while they themselves had lavished great care on the human child. A less drastic way of revealing a changeling's true identity is by engaging in behaviour that tricks it into giving itself away. In the 1850s, the German researcher Konrad Maurer recorded two versions of an Icelandic tale in which a farmer's wife deliberately behaves so strangely that the changeling becomes confused: the woman places a tiny pot on the hearth and tries to stir it with an absurdly long stick, causing the astonished changeling to exclaim: 'I'm as old as you can see from my beard and am the father of eighteen children, but I've never seen such a long whisk in such a small bowl.'

Stories about changelings are widespread in European traditions about elves and fairies. In Ireland – the subject of the next chapter – they even play a central role in the local narrative tradition. In Iceland, too, such tales are well documented, but are relatively rare within the overall picture; and in some regions they are not found at all. Moreover, such folktales sometimes include elements that are surprising within an Icelandic context. It is unclear, for example, why Icelandic elves should object to a cross on a cradle: in the overwhelming majority of surviving sources, the Hidden People of Iceland uphold the Christian faith and even have their own churches. Here, it is important to note how closely these narratives resemble Irish fairy legends: the impact of the

Christian symbols of salvation, the mistreatment of a changeling and even the idea of catching the changeling off guard by behaving strangely while cooking are – without exception – motifs that we shall encounter again when we turn to the Irish tradition. In all of these cases, the motifs in question appear to have been taken over from the Gaelic world and were never fully adapted to suit the new conditions in Iceland.

Central to all of the evidence about traditional Icelandic elves is the neighbourly relationship between humans and the Hidden People. Rural Iceland is characterized by a type of settlement largely consisting of isolated farmsteads. Even today there are few villages and towns in Iceland, and these emerged relatively late on in the island's history. In a country made up of dispersed settlements of this kind, human neighbours often live very far away. Conversely, the hills and rock formations that traditional storytellers identify as the homes of the Hidden People are mostly located in the immediate vicinity of the farmsteads. Since these elves employ the same agricultural methods as the human farmers, their lives are often closely interwoven both topographically and economically.

This close coexistence between elves and humans means that even in the twentieth century, many stories became attached to the area around individual Icelandic farms. A concrete example may serve to illustrate just how rich this narrative landscape can be. Map 1 shows the area surrounding the farm of Naustvík, which was remote even by Icelandic standards and which was abandoned in the 1960s, though its narrative tradition had already been documented in detail.

One of the stories about elves that is associated with this farm dates from the time when the last family of farmers took over the property in the middle of the nineteenth century. The family initially had very little money and no cattle, but one day they saw a cow lying on a rocky promontory to the east of the farm. This cow was visible in the morning, but by the afternoon it had vanished. The new farmer went over to the spit of land to find out what had happened to the animal, but found only a cowpat. The cow never came back and, since the nearest human neighbours lived a long way off, it was assumed that it had been a 'hidden cow' belonging to the local elves.

A generation later, there was further evidence of the elves' activities as dairy farmers. By now the farm was being run by the first farmer's daughter. A cow that had recently calved was producing milk only intermittently, and so she assumed that it was not being properly looked after. At that point she dreamt that a woman appeared to her, whom she did not know but who explained that no one at the farm was to blame for the cow's irregular lactation. Rather, the Hidden People who lived on the farm were currently in a predicament: both the husband and the son of the elf woman were seriously ill and her own cow had not yet calved, so it was not producing the milk that might have helped nurse the invalids back to health. The woman running the farm later had a second dream, in which the elf woman appeared to her once more, but this time she gave the impression that she was happy: her family, she explained, had recovered and her cow had calved, so they now had their own supply of milk. She also mentioned that they were still living in the rock formation at Snoppa, directly below the farm, but would soon be moving to Höfði. And with that she bade the woman a heartfelt farewell.

These two stories illustrate how small the distance may be between humans and elves on a farm: they live only a few minutes' walk apart and within sight of one another. They are engaged in the same kind of agriculture. And they live in equally modest circumstances, although in this story the

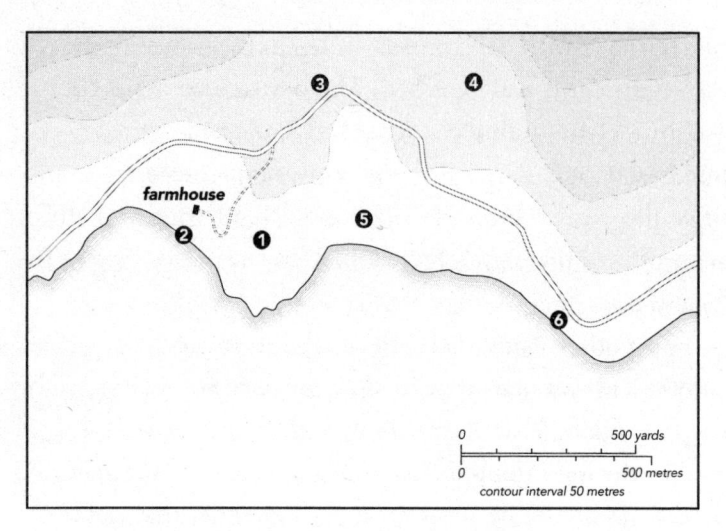

Map 1. The supernatural landscape surrounding the farm of Naustvík. The former farmhouse lies at the end of the driveway marked on the map. 1) Höfði, the rocky peninsula where an elf cow was seen; 2) the Snoppa rock formation, an elf home directly beneath the farmhouse; 3) Kirkjuklettur (Church Rock), the church of the Hidden People; 4) Grænuflöt (Green Lawn), a home of the Hidden People that humans were banned from mowing; 5) Flöskubakstóftir, the ruins haunted by a ghost called Bottle-Back; and 6) Tröllkarl, a petrified troll.

elves were initially slightly better off, albeit not sufficiently wealthy to be able to manage without human assistance. In this way 'hidden agriculture' turns out, in essence, to be a mirror image of human agrarian activity. The second story also shows that tales about Hidden People played a role in the humans' dealings with one another: the dream in which the elf woman appears helps to explain a situation in which the woman running the farm has started to suspect that someone on the farm is mistreating a cow, which represents an essential part of the farmstead's resources. A situation like this not only constitutes an economic burden, it also gives rise to mistrust and resentment in an environment in which humans have to live and work together very closely, if they are to deal with life's daily challenges. The elf woman's appearance in a dream offered an alternative explanation for the cow's irregular lactation – an irregularity for which no one at the farm was to blame. In this way it provided an opportunity to resolve a tense situation and restore peace to the farm. Equally typical is the dynamic between the sexes: these dreams are often found in tales about Icelandic elves, and the person who has the dream is generally an older woman who can then exercise her authority with the support of the Hidden People. We do not know exactly how this episode with the cow unfolded in real life, but it is at least tempting to suppose that the story about the plight of the elves on the farm was intended to end an argument over who had failed to look after the farmstead's only milch cow.

In short, the lives of the Naustvík elves were closely interwoven with life on the farm. But equally close was their connection with the land on which the farm was situated. I have so far mentioned two places at Naustvík associated with elves: the rocks at Snoppa and Höfði. These rock formations were no more than 50 metres and 250 metres, respectively, from the farmhouse, in this way illustrating the extreme density of these elfin settlements (Illus. 3). And Snoppa and Höfði were by no means the only places on the farm that were associated with elves. Some 450 metres above the farmhouse, the coastal road met an old bridle path, and here it is still possible to see a rock by the name of Kirkjuklettur (Church Rock). This rock formation looks like a masonry wall and is said to have been the church of the Hidden People (Illus. 4). A further 400 metres to the east of the elves' church was Grænuflöt (Green Lawn), a small stretch of grassland that is surprisingly flat and that is situated on a mountain spur, where elves lived and where humans were discouraged from cutting the grass, as this was a forbidden place of the *álagablettur* kind. In other words, there were no fewer than four places associated with elves within a radius

3. A view of the Bay of Naustvík with the old farmhouse and the elf dwellings of Snoppa and Höfði immediately beneath and beyond the farm.

4. The elf church Kirkjuklettur (Church Rock).

of only a few hundred metres, all of them located on land belonging to the farm: at three of these places elves were said to live, while the fourth was the location of a church. One of these places was additionally a forbidden area. Not even these constituted the sum total of otherworld presences on this parcel of farmland, for on the coast to the east of the farm, beyond the elf rock on the promontory at Höfði, are some ruins known as Flöskubakstóftir (Bottle-Back Ruins) and said to be haunted by the ghost Bottle-Back. This ghost carried a collection of bottles on his back, their clinking and rattling always announcing his approach. Furthermore, beyond the haunted ruins is a stone pillar that, according to legend, is a male troll who had been surprised by the rising sun and turned to stone. From then until the end of time he stares across to the other side of the fjord, where a female troll had suffered a similar fate.

In short, the land surrounding the farm is filled with otherworld creatures, elves playing a dominant, but by no means exclusive, role here. The high density of this otherworld settlement is all the more striking in that the human population hereabouts is distinctly thin on the ground. The Naustvík farm has multiple elfin neighbours within a radius of only a few hundred metres – in some cases significantly less – whereas the nearest human neighbours on the fjord were a good 5 kilometres away. The Icelandic folklorist Einar Ólafur Sveinsson interpreted the ideas about the Hidden People in precisely this context as long ago as 1940. He noticed that many of the stories about elves in Iceland give the impression that, in their loneliness and longing for human contact, the locals cried out to nature until the rocks and hills opened up and filled with Hidden People. Even today, Iceland's extremely low population density makes this one of the most convincing interpretations of the essential nature of the island's Hidden

People. The stories about these elves have many aspects to them and were used in fundamentally different ways in Iceland's traditional rural culture, but their decisive feature appears to be the desire to fill the oppressively vast emptiness of an inhospitable land with at least a semblance of human society designed to mitigate people's isolation – if not in real life, then at least in their imagination. The fact that this idea is rooted in the emptiness of the country may also be one of the reasons why notions about the Hidden People have changed so dramatically in the urban environment of the Reykjavík metropolitan area in recent decades. This is a point to which we shall return in a later chapter.

CHAPTER 2

ELVES IN GAELIC IRELAND

The vast expanse of the Atlantic Ocean separates Iceland from Europe, and yet this same ocean also forged a link between them. The Icelandic *Landnámabók* (*Book of Settlements*) lays great emphasis on this point. This is a medieval text dating from the twelfth or thirteenth century and describing how Iceland was first settled in the ninth and tenth centuries. According to this text, it took five days to sail from Ireland, the nearest major European land mass, to Iceland, and the journey was undertaken not only by Norse settlers, but also by Irish people, so the earliest settlers in Iceland were a mixture of Scandinavians and Gaelic speakers from Scotland and Ireland. An important factor in this context was a more general westward expansion of Scandinavians in the ninth and tenth centuries – the Age of the Vikings – when Scandinavia extended its sphere of influence through both aggressive expansionism and peaceful trade. In the course of this expansion, Scandinavian colonies were established in Scotland and Ireland, as well as in smaller archipelagos, such as the Shetland Isles and the Faroes. This development culminated in the settlement of Iceland, starting in the 850s. In other words, Iceland was settled not directly from Scandinavia, but by many arrivals who had already spent some time in Ireland and Scotland before embarking on a second stage of their journey and moving on to Iceland.

The *Book of Settlements*' description of the life of one of the most famous settlers is a good example of the dynamics of this period. Auðr *djúpauðga* (Audr the Deep-Minded) came from the highest echelons of Nordic society, members of which established themselves in Ireland and Scotland during these years. Her husband was the king of Dublin, and at the height of his power her son is said to have governed large parts of Scotland. Only when both men had fallen in battle did Auðr set off with her followers in a westerly direction and settle in Iceland. Among these followers were many Irish and Scots, and even the members of her immediate family spoke at least a smattering of Gaelic, the Celtic language of Ireland and Scotland. In other words, the earliest settlers to establish a colony in Iceland were not only Scandinavians, but also people from Ireland and Scotland, while even the Scandinavian settlers had often been exposed to the influence of the Gaelic language and Gaelic culture.

This early and intense Gaelic influence on Iceland explains why there are such striking similarities between the traditional elves of Iceland and those of Ireland. In both cases, the world of the elves is often located underground and inside mounds and rocks. Here they live in an alternative, otherworld space, but without being completely cut off from the human world. In neither Iceland nor Ireland is the world of the elves a unified otherworld shut off from the world of humans. Rather, elves live in a variety of places closely interconnected with the human landscape: the mounds and other places where elves live lie scattered across the world inhabited by humans, and each of these elfin mounds is a world unto itself. Various very specific stories about elves were also recounted in both Iceland and Ireland, and we shall later return in more detail to an Irish variant of one of the Icelandic tales mentioned in the previous chapter.

Even so, the elves of Iceland and of the Gaelic world – in other words, Ireland and Scotland – are by no means identical. In many respects, Irish 'elves' have their own distinctive character, quite apart from which ideas and stories about these creatures changed in the course of the centuries. The early part of this chapter will focus on the literature of the early and High Middle Ages – from the eighth to the fourteenth centuries – while the latter part will examine the very different type of elves of the later period and, more especially, the elves of the nineteenth and twentieth centuries.

Ireland in the Middle Ages: The Tribes of the Goddess Danu

Medieval Ireland has a long literary tradition in which the supernatural beings of the autochthonous otherworld play an unusually large role, even when compared to the other literatures of medieval Europe. In the Gaelic language, the 'fairies' that are found in these texts are generally called *Túatha Dé* (tribes of the gods), *Túatha Dé Danann* (tribes of the goddess Danu) or *áes síde* (people of the fairy mounds). The reference to 'tribes' is a reflection of the political organization of medieval Ireland, which was divided into countless small communities and, as such, found its exact counterpart in an equally fragmented otherworld. True, medieval Ireland was ruled by a high king whose reign extended to the whole of Ireland, but on a local level, the country was governed by a hundred or so lesser kings. In much the same way, in theory the Túatha Dé were subject to the authority of a common ruler, at least according to a number of texts, whereas in practice they lived in largely independent 'elf mounds'. These mounds – often prehistoric burial mounds, but also sometimes natural mounds – do not mark the entrance to a single otherworld, but are always independent entities. In other words, Irish literature does not acknowledge the existence of a single otherworld, but of a multiplicity of these hidden worlds, each of which has its own location within the actual landscape.

An early example of one such otherworld may date back to the eighth century. *De Gabáil in t-Ṡída* (*Concerning the Seizure of the Fairy Mound*) tells of a mighty king who once ruled over the Túatha Dé in Ireland – the Dagda. He was so powerful that he was able to rob humans of their harvests and milk yields, forcing them to enter into a bond of friendship with him. He would then protect their crops and their milk. His power over the Túatha Dé was initially uncontested, so it was he who allotted their fairy mounds to the various members of the Túatha Dé. His own mound was the Síd in Broga, which is the Neolithic grave mound of Newgrange in the valley of the Boyne, to the north of Dublin (Illus. 5). But one of the most prominent members of the Irish otherworld, the Mac Óc, was left empty-handed when these fairy mounds were distributed. In order to ensure that he too had a mound, the Mac Óc had recourse to a cunning ruse that involved him asking the Dagda, who had overlooked him when distributing these mounds, to lend him the Síd in Broga for a day and a night. The Dagda agreed and handed over his mound to the Mac Óc, but when he asked for it back after a day and a night, the Mac Óc replied that time in general consists of day and night,

5. The Neolithic grave mound of Newgrange in the valley of the Boyne.

which is precisely what the Dagda had agreed to. The Dagda had to admit defeat and relinquished his mound to the Mac Óc. One version of the text ends with a description of the interior of the mound:

> Wonderful, moreover, [is] that land. Three trees with fruit are there always, and a pig eternally alive, and a roasted swine, and a vessel with marvelous liquor, and never do they all decrease.[1]

Although brief, *Concerning the Seizure of the Fairy Mound* contains a whole series of motifs that are typical of the Túatha Dé of medieval Irish literature. The Túatha Dé have power over the agricultural yield (crops and milk) and, hence, the staple diet of humans. They dwell in places, especially mounds, in the actual Irish landscape. The world within these mounds is notable for its wondrous and never-ending abundance of food, with particular emphasis on the expensive dishes and drinks associated with the aristocracy: apples, pork and a wondrous beverage. Most of these motifs continue to reverberate in Irish folktales of the early twentieth century.

Even though the concept of the *síd* as a fairy mound permeates the whole of Irish literature, the interior of these mounds is not the only place where the otherworld is said to be located: sometimes it is underwater, on an island in a lake, or even in the west, on the furthest side of the ocean. One of the oldest surviving tales in the Irish language is *Echtrae Chonnlai* (*Connle's Journey to the Otherworld*, also known as *Connle's Adventure*), which dates back to the years around 700 and tells how Connle, the son of the Irish high king Conn of the Hundred Battles, was lured away by a fairy maiden to her otherworld.

This woman suddenly appears to Connle when he and his father are standing beside one of the central sites in the history of the high kings of Ireland. She explains to him that

> I come from the Lands of the Living, where there is neither death nor want nor sin. We keep perpetual feast without need for service. Peace (*síd*) reigns among us without strife. A great fairy-mound/peace (*síd*) it is, in which we live; wherefore we are called 'folk of the fairy-mound/of peace' (*áes síde*).[2]

She then declares her love for Connle and invites him to join her at Mag Mell (Plain of Delights), where he will neither grow old nor die, but will continue to enjoy eternal youth until the Day of Judgement. The king bids his druids drive the woman away; but before she leaves, she throws Connle an apple. For a whole month he eats nothing but this apple, which remains exactly the same size, no matter how much of it he consumes. When the woman returns a month later and again invites Connle to accompany her back to the Land of Eternal Youth, he decides with a heavy heart to abandon his family and leave with the fairy. His family tries to prevent him, but Connle manages to elude them and sails away with his otherworld love on a crystalline ship that takes them over the sea. He has never been heard of since.

In *Connle's Journey to the Otherworld*, the otherworld is described as a paradise that shares many features with the world of the Dagda's fairy mound. Both texts stress the plentiful supply of food in the otherworld: in the Dagda's fairy mound there are wondrous fruit trees that always bear fruit. Similarly, the apple that sustains Connle for a whole month is never depleted. In the mound there is always something to drink and a roast pig that never grows less. In the fairy's otherworld, 'we keep perpetual feast without need for service'. The paradisal nature of this otherworld is underscored by the fairy by means of a play on words involving the term *áes síde*, a phrase frequently used to describe the 'folk of the fairy mound' and made up of two elements, *áes* (folk) and *síd* (fairy mound). But Old Irish also has a homonym, *síd*, meaning 'peace', and it is to this that the fairy refers when she tells Connle that she lives 'in a great fairy mound/ in great peace', so they are called 'folk of the fairy mound/ peace'. Yet there is a fundamental difference here, inasmuch as this fairy's otherworld paradise lies not inside a mound, but on the other side of the sea.

A number of Irish texts offer us the possibility of locating the otherworld beyond the sea. Apart from *Connle's Journey to the Otherworld*, the best-known reworking of this motif is to be found in *Immram Brain* (*Bran's Sea Voyage*), which is likewise believed to date from around 700. Here, too, a nobleman – in this case, King Bran – encounters a woman from the otherworld who invites him to join her in a land of eternal youth located beyond the sea. Bran, too, never returns, although in his case he does at least attempt to do so. He leaves for the otherworld in a ship with his royal retinue. After they have stayed for some time in the otherworld, one of his companions is overcome by homesickness and Bran sails back to Ireland. When they reach land, his companion leaps out of the ship, only to turn to dust the moment he touches Irish soil – it is as if he has lain in his grave for centuries. The otherworld represents a permanent temptation, but time there passes at a different rate, with the result that even in the oldest Irish texts it is often already impossible to return to the land of mortals.

This notion that in the otherworld time operates according to different rules is central to *Echtra Nerai* (*Nera's Journey to the Otherworld*), a tale that stresses the dangers of an aspect that is merely hinted at in *Connle's Journey to the Otherworld* and in *Bran's Sea Voyage*. It is difficult to determine exactly when *Nera's Journey to the Otherworld* was written – the most likely date is sometime between the eighth and the tenth century. The story begins at the dead of night on Samain, the festival marking the beginning of winter on 31 October/1 November – a date when, according to the Irish narrative tradition, the boundaries between the human world and other worlds are at their most porous. The court of Connacht has gathered round King Ailill and Queen Medb in the hall of the royal palace at Crúachan. The previous evening two prisoners had been hanged. King Ailill presents his assembled warriors with a challenge: anyone who manages to tie a twig round one of the dead men's legs will receive a prize. One warrior after another goes outside into the pitch-black night, but returns to his seat very quickly. Finally, Nera accepts the challenge. He goes outside and tries to tie a twig round one of the dead men's legs; but it keeps springing back, until the dead man on the gallows tells him to attach it by means of a peg. Nera follows his advice and this time the twig stays in place. The dead man then asks Nera to carry him to a house where he can find something to drink, adding that he had been thirsty when he was hanged. Nera lifts the man onto his back and carries him off to a series of houses. The dead man is unable to enter the first two of them, because the fire has been properly banked for the night and the water that the people had used to wash themselves in has been thrown away, so these two houses are protected by lakes of fire and water. Not until they reach the third house does the dead man find a drink, the occupants having gone to bed without taking out the dirty water, which they have left standing in buckets and washtubs. The dead man drinks some of the dirty water and spits the rest over the faces of the sleeping occupants, killing them all. Nera then carries him back to the gallows.

On his return to the palace, Nera finds a scene of devastation awaiting him: the buildings have all been burnt down and the decapitated heads of the courtiers tossed onto a pile. Nera is just in time to see the assailants riding away: an army from the fairy mound. Nera sets off in pursuit. After passing through the Cave of Crúachan (Illus. 6), the warriors reach the fairy mound, or *síd*, where they live. But Nera has been spotted. When the warriors appear before their king inside the mound, Nera, too, is presented to him, together with the heads that his army has brought back as spoils of war. The fairy king orders Nera to move in with a single woman and perform menial tasks for the king.

Nera and the fairy with whom he has been told to live soon become a couple and she tells him that not everything

6. The Cave of Crúachan, an entrance to the otherworld.

is as it appears to be. The destruction of the royal palace at Crúachan that Nera thinks he has seen will not, in fact, take place until Samain the following year – and only then if Nera does not go back to Crúachan to warn King Ailill and Queen Medb.

It is at this stage in the narrative that the difference in the way in which time is measured in the otherworld becomes particularly apparent. Nera thinks that he has spent several days in the fairy mound, but in the world of humans, Ailill and Medb are still eating the same meal as the one that Nera had left. The fairy explains this dislocation between human time and time as measured in the otherworld, and gives him the means by which to convince the assembled court that his tale is true. In the world of humans it is winter, but in the fairy mound it is summer, so the fairy gives Nera some summer herbs that he can use to prove the truth of what he has witnessed. Nera returns to his king and queen, tells them of his adventure and warns them of the danger they are in. Further complications follow, but in the end the court is ready to fend off an attack by the fairy army. Instead of being butchered, the humans, led by the king, plunder the fairy mound and carry off valuable treasures, including the crown of Brión that later belonged to the Uí Briúin clan (which was in power in Connacht at the time the story was written). But Nera decides to remain with his lover in her fairy mound. He has not re-emerged since returning to it.

The tale of Nera's adventure is typical of many of the central features of the world of the *síde* or fairy mounds. This otherworld is very different, while also mirroring the world of human society and the latter's aristocratic order. It is both alluring and dangerous: the otherworld contains great treasures and holds out the promise of love and eternal life, but it can also destroy the world of human beings. A very specific feature is the way in which time passes at a very different rate inside a fairy mound: past and future merge and the seasons do not follow their normal course. The time that is spent in the otherworld does not count as it would in the human world, and obeys very different rules.

In the Ireland and Scotland of the Middle Ages, these various elements led to the emergence of a kind of literature whose influence reached far beyond the confines of the specifically Gaelic world. A good example of this extended impact is the tale of Nera's adventure. To prove to the court at Crúachan that his story is true, Nera is advised by the fairy to take plants that flower in summer to the wintry world of humans. A parallel story is found in the *Gesta Danorum* that Saxo Grammaticus wrote in Denmark in the years around 1200. Here Saxo tells a story about King Hadingus, who is sitting down for a meal when a woman suddenly appears from out of the ground. Although it is around the time of the winter solstice, she is carrying the sort of fresh flowers normally seen only in summer. She asks the king if he knows where such flowers can be found in the depths of winter. This piques the king's curiosity and he agrees to go with her on a visit to a subterranean otherworld. The tales of the Norse King Hadingus and the Irish warrior Nera share a number of striking details: in both of them, a woman from an underground otherworld uses summer herbs during a banquet in winter to convince the members of a human court that the otherworld really exists; and in both cases the king sets off on a journey to this otherworld – in one instance on his own, in the other at the head of an army. This is only one of several examples of the way in which tales from the world of Gaelic literature could become known – and even loved – far beyond their original borders.

The aforementioned examples of Irish tales about the otherworld of the *síd* and the Túatha Dé Danann all date from the early Middle Ages, but this is a narrative tradition that has remained unbroken right down to the present day. From the eighteenth century there has survived a hugely influential poem with the title *Laoidh Oisín ar Thír na nÓg* (*The Lay of Oisín in the Land of the Young/Ageless*), which describes the Land of Youth – the Tír na nÓg – as a place which, like the others already summarized, lies outside the laws of time as measured by human beings.

The tale's tragic hero is Oisín, one of the leaders of a band of mythic warriors that played an important role in Irish literature over a period of several centuries. Taking a folktale as its starting point, the poem tells how the prehistoric hero Oisín once met Saint Patrick, who converted Ireland to Christianity several centuries after Oisín's time. Of decisive importance for bridging the centuries between the times of the two men is Niamh, the daughter of the king of Tír na nÓg. Niamh loves Oisín, and so she mounts a magnificent white horse and rides to the world of mortals to take Oisín back with her to Tír na nÓg. As soon as he sees her and she speaks to him, he is fired by feelings of love and, leaping onto her stallion, rides back to the otherworld with her, heading westwards over the ocean.

The poem describes this otherworld in great detail, depicting it as a paradise of incredible beauty and abundance, where no one grows old and its inhabitants retain their youth for ever. Oisín is happy here for three centuries, but is then overwhelmed by a desire to see his old comrades again. It is only with great reluctance that Niamh allows Oisín to leave since she suspects that he will never return. She lends him her white horse and makes it clear to him that he must never touch Irish soil, otherwise it will then be impossible for him to come back to her. Oisín rides over the ocean to Ireland, but barely recognizes it: in the three centuries he has been away, the country has changed and its inhabitants are now all stunted and weak in comparison to the heroes of yore. From the people he meets, Oisín discovers that he himself is no more than a character in a legend that tells how a hero was spirited away by a woman from the otherworld and taken to the Land of the Young. Oisín scours the whole of Ireland in search of his old companions, but all trace of them has vanished. He finally abandons his search and sets off back to the Land of the Young. But on the way, he encounters a group of men attempting to move a large stone. Oisín finds their attempts ridiculous, because the heroes of his own generation would have been able to lift such a stone with only one hand. So he leans down from his saddle to help them. But his saddle girth snaps and he falls to the ground, at which point the intervening centuries catch up with him. The white horse returns without him to the Land of the Young, while Oisín remains behind, an old, blind man who has reached the end of his life.

The Fairy World of Irish Folktales: The Good People

By its very nature, the medieval evidence of the existence of the 'people of the fairy mounds' is literary and, as such, a product of the highest echelons of Irish society. Within the written tradition, these tales express the interests of predominantly male clerics and aristocrats. The great significance that is attached by the texts to food production and to the abundance of food in the otherworld reflects the fact that in the early Middle Ages, the upper reaches of Irish society had a largely rural mindset and were closely bound up with agrarian concerns: essentially, a medieval aristocrat was a landowner. Nevertheless, the voice of the 'simple folk' is not heard in these works. It is not until the nineteenth century that the rich narrative tradition of the lower orders of society and of its poorer members emerges with any clarity. This tradition is no longer elitist and no longer confined to the written word, but is oral and bound up with the cares of people whose lives are dominated by want and by sheer hard work.

Despite the great social changes that took place over the intervening centuries, there nonetheless remains an astonishing sense of continuity between the Middle Ages and the nineteenth- and twentieth-century tradition. During the 1930s, the Republic of Ireland's Irish Folklore Commission embarked on a large-scale initiative that involved gathering records of folk customs and tales, when primary schoolchildren collected and wrote down the fairytales and legends recounted by their parents, grandparents and neighbours. This initiative alone – and it was only one of multiple strategies designed to record Irish folk traditions – produced some 740,000 pages of documentation immortalizing Irish traditions.

One detail that recurs with striking frequency in these records is the care that is taken in disposing of water used for personal ablutions. Time and time again it is stressed in these documents that the 'old folk' used to be very concerned to ensure that the water they had used to get washed in was removed from the house each evening before the occupants went to bed, because otherwise the building would invite the attention of the spirits of the dead – English-language sources specifically use the word 'fairies' here. Precisely the same thing is found in the early medieval tale of *Nera's Journey to the Otherworld*: a dead man can enter a building at night only if it still contains the water with which the occupants had washed themselves earlier that day. This leads in turn to the death of everyone in the building. A thousand years after *Nera's Journey to the Otherworld* first found written form, an almost identical story was still being told in nineteenth-century Ireland, replicating a narrative that had already assumed its first literary form in the early Middle Ages.

Despite these continuities, modern tales about fairies often have a very different underlying tenor from that found in the Middle Ages. While medieval literature tells of heroes and kings, modern accounts often speak of the sufferings of the impoverished rural population. This change is already reflected in the terminology used to describe the 'fairies': in modern folktales they are no longer said to be members of the Túatha Dé or *áes síde*, but have a multiplicity of names, most of which seem to be intended to express no name at all, the aim apparently being not to draw the attention of these creatures to the speaker. Among the terms used in the recent past have been *daoine maithe* (Good People), *bunadh na gcnoc* (people of the mounds), *daoine beaga* (Little People) and *na huaisle* (the Gentry). Conversely, the specific term *síogaí* (fairies), which is cognate with Old Irish *síd*, is used only relatively rarely.

This use of circumlocutions for the Good People appears to imply a certain respectful inhibition, a quality apparent not only on a linguistic level, but also – and even more clearly – within the tales themselves. A good example of this is the way in which the motif of the white horse is used in modern folktales. We have already encountered this motif in the *Lay of Oisín in the Land of the Young*, where the horse carries the hero on his journey to, and tragic return from, the otherworld. Lady Gregory (Illus. 7), who began collecting folktales in the West of Ireland in the 1890s, documented several variants of a story with a recurrent underlying structure: a woman is abducted and taken to fairyland; she appears to her husband in a vision and informs him that – either on her own or within a group of fairies – she will ride on a (generally white) horse to a certain place, where he can find her and win her back. In one of the versions of this tale, the husband follows his wife's instructions and rescues her from the fairies' grip. In another version, the husband loses heart at the very last moment and, without making any attempt to rescue his wife, allows the fairy band to ride away with her. And in a third version, the wife instructs her husband not to come in person, but to send his brother instead. Although the brother manages to rescue her, he dies within a week, while the rescued wife lives a long life, but is unable to string three words together to form a coherent sentence. All of these tales focus on the threat that is represented by the Good People.

The type of tale that involves a wife's abduction also introduces us to a motif that played a key role in Irish fairy stories and in the popular belief in fairies in nineteenth-century Ireland: the changeling. Many Irish fairy stories revolve around the idea that little children, women in labour and healthy young people in general are the preferred victims of the Good People when it comes to their abduction. These victims do not simply

7. Lady Isabella Augusta Gregory.

disappear, however, but are replaced by a changeling that the Good People leave in their stead. Such a changeling is a mere shadow of the abducted person. While the individuals who have been spirited away were in the prime of life, the changelings are wizened and feeble, mostly bedridden and often mentally impaired. Alternatively, the people who are abducted are replaced by something that appears to be their lifeless body. But after the person has been buried, anyone who harbours any suspicions and who insists on reopening the coffin will find not the mortal remains of the person in question, but only a piece of wood or a broom. Tales about these changelings often stress the fact that it is the finest, healthiest and strongest members of the local community who are taken: the Good People abduct those who they think will be of the most use to them, leaving in their place old creatures that they don't know what to do with. The result is that the changelings left behind do nothing but eat and demand attention, making the lives of those who have lost a loved one even harder than before. For the Good People in these folktales, the individuals who have been abducted provide new blood and considerable help as manual labourers. It was often said that women who died in childbirth were needed as wet-nurses for the children born in the fairy world. On the other hand, old men and women were never abducted because, as one old man on the Aran Islands asked Lady Gregory: 'What would they do with them?'

The ideas about fairies that circulated in nineteenth-century Ireland were a way of dealing with the frequent deaths that weighed heavily on a society with little access to medical help and which was already weakened by poverty and famine. More especially in the Gaelic-speaking parts of the West of Ireland, the population suffered from the consequences of a poor diet and had only the most limited access to what nineteenth-century medicine could offer. There was a high infant mortality rate, and death in childbirth was a constant and very real danger. Even people in the best of health could contract an infection and die for apparently no reason, or become bedridden. The idea of being abducted by fairies seems to have served as a mechanism that offered the survivors a chance to invest the serious consequences of such tragedies with at least a semblance of meaning and explain these otherwise senseless sufferings.

This function of these fairy stories emerges with particular clarity from a comparison between two collections that owed their existence to differing circumstances. In Lady Gregory's anthology, which dates from the 1890s onwards, those changelings that are left behind after the human children have been abducted are always described in a way that makes it apparent that we are dealing with the victims of severe depression or of illnesses and accidents that have rendered them bedridden. It was the consequences of a deficient health system that held up the Good People as a plausible explanation. Another extensive collection of fairy stories was compiled by Seán Ó hEochaidh in the fishing villages of Donegal in the 1930s, 1940s and 1950s. Here, too, life was hard, but death in childbirth and the sort of illnesses that led to people being bedridden for long periods were no longer as prevalent as they had been in Lady Gregory's day. The fishing families of the 1930s, conversely, were more exercised by the dangers of the sea and by the fear of dying at sea. It was these dangers and fears, therefore, that were central to the local fairy stories.

Traditional accounts of the Good People provided not only 'explanations' but also various strategies for defending oneself against them. In this way, the tales offered at least a sense of certainty and the possibility of help in confronting the psychological pressure of lives spent in permanent uncertainty. In consequence, the Good People could be driven away by iron, salt or fire, or by invoking God and His saints. All of these elements were omnipresent in rural life and were able to provide protection against daily dangers and uncertainties. To take an example: an iron nail placed in a cradle could protect the infant and prevent it from being snatched away by the Good People. Translated into today's thought patterns, this implies that the nail gave the child's parents the hope that it would not die suddenly in infancy or suffer the consequences of the numerous illnesses that were untreatable at that time.

There was another area, too, in which fairy stories gave contemporaries a chance to speak a language that allowed them to deal with suffering and misfortune. Many of the fairy stories from the nineteenth century tell of men and women who are abducted only briefly by the Good People and who, on their return, report having seen various dead villagers leading good lives among the fairy folk. In particular, many of the young women who had died in childbirth were not actually dead, but were dwelling among the Good People and enjoying greater wealth and affluence than they could ever have hoped for in the world of humankind. Like the medieval world of the *áes síde*, the world of the Good People in the nineteenth and early twentieth centuries was still a place of relative wealth and abundance. One tale that Lady Gregory was told by a certain Mrs Sheridan describes a vision, in which the fairies' local habitat was said to resemble the manor house of a major English landowner: it was like a scene of the greatest imaginable wealth in local human society.

At the same time, the fairy tradition opened up the possibility of people clinging onto hope, even in the knowledge that there was none. Time and again, Irish fairy stories tell how it is possible for abducted individuals to be brought back to the world of mortals – frequently after a period of seven years. The stories often give the impression of being an attempt on the part of those who are caring for the incurably sick to instil themselves with a sense of hope that the invalid may yet recover. At the same time, examples such as the tale of the woman on a white horse also make it clear that people were perfectly aware that such hope was unrealistic.

But even unrealistic hopes can serve a purpose in society. Among the traditions collected by Lady Gregory from the late nineteenth century onwards we find repeated instances of the idea that people who have been abducted may still come back, as long as they manage not to eat any of the fairies' food – for only after people have tasted the food from the otherworld are they lost for good. In some tales, this idea is combined with the explicit demand that a small amount of food be placed outside the houses of humans every evening, because in this way the people who have been abducted will be able to eat human food and not lose their one last hope of returning to the world of humans.

Behind the mythical picture that is found in these tales of changelings one can sense a kind of poor relief: in a society that had practically no system of social insurance, there were always people in need who depended on this kind of food aid. The description of these food donations in fairy stories, with their particularly vivid imagery, meant that those in need did not have to go begging and ensured that they had regular minimal provisions. This was a response to the social needs of the time. And the fairy stories changed as those needs changed: by the time Seán Ó hEochaidh collected his own set of fairy stories in the 1930s, the situation had markedly improved, with the result that his collection contains no further examples of this kind of poor relief.

Alongside these positive aspects, however, we also find acts of extreme brutality – acts that could be legitimized by the nineteenth century's ideas about fairies. One of the women who provided Lady Gregory with her own traditions about fairies was a policeman's wife. She told Lady Gregory about a case in which her husband had been involved. A woman in County Clare had become obsessed by the idea that her daughter was a changeling. In order to get her 'real' child back, she used a method that is often mentioned in tales about changelings: she lit a fire in the middle of her cottage and placed her little daughter on the red-hot coals, in the belief that this would drive away the changeling and restore her own daughter to her. Hearing the little girl's screams, one of the neighbours came running, the police were called and the mother was arrested. But the magistrate who presided over the trial dismissed the case against the woman on the grounds that she was uneducated and had done only what she thought was right.

There are several instances of such child abuse and infanticide in Irish court records, all of them involving attempts to drive out a changeling and win back the 'real' child. Few of the perpetrators were punished, the majority of magistrates treating the crimes as instances of local superstitions that, as a rule, they felt should be tolerated. One of the unspoken reasons for this rationale may have been the view that in such cases these traditional fairy stories served to rationalize the killing of sick or handicapped children when a poor family, for want of welfare and health services, had been driven to the point of total collapse: the unspeakable and the unbearable could be put into words in the form of a fairy legend.

The limits of what society was prepared to tolerate at this time are clear from the case of the murder of the twenty-six-year-old Bridget Cleary, who, by the standards of her day, was an unusually independent woman with her own profession and her own income. She lived with her husband Michael Cleary in County Tipperary and worked as a seamstress. In March 1895, she fell seriously ill and was confined to bed for several days, during which time her family and her neighbours feared for her life. Indeed, her condition deteriorated to the point where the local priest gave her the last rites. In parallel with the Church's official reaction, traditional ideas about fairies developed their own dynamics in an attempt to deal with the crisis. Once the last rites had been administered, a group of Bridget's relatives and acquaintances embarked on a series of measures derived from traditional tales about changelings and designed to drive out the supposed changeling and persuade the fairies to return the strong and healthy Bridget, in place of her sickly, dying counterpart. In addition to her illness, Bridget now had to endure the sort of procedures associated with identifying and expelling a changeling. She was forced to drink a broth brewed from herbs; was drenched in urine – said to drive away fairies; and was ritually threatened with being exposed to the fire on the hearth. Despite all this, she recovered and, after a few days, was able to get up from her sickbed.

It was at this juncture, however, that events got out of hand. Michael and Bridget Cleary became involved in an argument over the changeling procedure, ending with Michael striking down his wife and burning her body. After that he became increasingly obsessed with the world of ideas related to changelings, tried to borrow a rifle and joined forces with two other men to stand guard at Kylenagranagh Fort, a place where fairies were said to live. Here he planned to rescue his wife when, astride a grey horse, she rode out from fairyland with the other fairies. For three nights he kept watch by the fairy fortress. The next day the Royal Irish Constabulary arrived with orders to arrest him.

The ensuing trial made international headlines (Illus. 8), not least because Bridget Cleary's murder had taken place at a time when the question of Irish self-rule was being hotly debated throughout the British Empire. The case served as ammunition for the pro-British party, which asked if a country could really rule itself when its inhabitants believed in fairies and went around murdering people for allegedly being changelings. The trial lasted several months and ended

8. The Bridget Cleary case, as illustrated in *The Daily Graphic* (1895).

with eight of the relatives and neighbours being found guilty. Michael Cleary was sentenced to twenty years' imprisonment, and six other men received sentences of between six months and five years. The oldest defendant was an elderly woman who – though she was found guilty – was spared prison on account of her years. Thanks to this trial, the murder of Bridget Cleary became the most significant example of how traditional ideas about fairies can turn into something altogether more dangerous in small rural communities that are under enormous economic and social pressure.

For all that the national and international attention it attracted suggested otherwise, the murder of Bridget Cleary was quite an exceptional way of dealing with the issue of changelings. At the opposite end of the spectrum we find a large number of tales and legends behind which lies nothing more than a sheer delight in storytelling. This playfulness is central to the story of the 'Brewery of Eggshells', which first appeared in print in 1825 in *Fairy Legends and Traditions of the South of Ireland*, a collection of stories edited by Thomas Crofton Croker and immediately translated into German by the Brothers Grimm, no less, in their *Irische Elfenmärchen* (*Irish Fairytales*) of 1826. (See also Chapter 5.)

In this story, a certain Mrs Sullivan suspects that her baby, which until recently has been perfectly healthy, has been replaced by a shrivelled old changeling. In order to test her suspicions, she takes a wise woman's advice and sets a trap for the creature, boiling some water in a large cauldron and then cracking some eggs. But instead of the yolks and egg whites, she throws only the shells into the boiling water. The creature forgets itself – after all, it should be playing the part of an infant not yet able to speak – and asks in astonishment what the woman is doing, to which Mrs Sullivan replies that she is brewing eggshells. At this point the changeling claps its hands together and exclaims: 'I'm fifteen hundred years in the world, and I never saw a brewery of egg-shells before.' Mrs Sullivan is about to attack the changeling with a red-hot poker and boiling water when the creature realizes its mistake and vanishes. In the cradle lies Mrs Sullivan's child once again.

It is presumably no accident that the changeling in this Irish fairytale behaves in exactly the same way as the one in the Icelandic anecdote that gave itself away by declaring that the lady of the house was stirring a tiny pot with an exaggeratedly long ladle. Variants of this tale are familiar from large parts of Western and Northern Europe. The changeling often gives itself away by noting that the other person is cooking using an eggshell, which in the Icelandic variant becomes a tiny pot. Ever since the early Middle Ages there had been regular traffic between Iceland and the Gaelic world of Ireland and Scotland and their neighbours, contact that finds expression not least in the close parallels that can be identified in the traditional tales that circulated in those countries. If the various versions of the 'Brewery of Eggshells' tale are so widely disseminated, then this is a reflection of those close intercultural links.

But it is not only in terms of specific tales that Ireland and Iceland resemble one another: the close link between narrative traditions and the landscape that we noted in the chapter on Iceland is also found in the case of Ireland. One example of this was documented in Kilcurry in County Louth in the 1890s (see Map 2). According to the local inhabitants, this tiny town was surrounded by places filled with fairies and ghosts: within a radius of no more than 2 kilometres, the Gentry – fairies – had three dwelling places and two roads, and alongside them there also were four well-documented ghostly apparitions. Faughart Church, a few hundred metres from Kilcurry, had been built in the early nineteenth century on the site of a prehistoric fort that was rumoured to have been inhabited by fairies. Once work on the church was in progress, the local fairies are said to have expressed their displeasure by conjuring up a false vision, in the course of which the workmen saw the church go up in flames. But this vision was the best that the fairies could manage in terms of preventing the work on the church from going ahead.

There were two other sites south of Kilcurry where fairies were said to live. Both were connected to the main road and were also linked to each other by two well-established fairy roads, most of which ran underground. There were also eyewitness reports of fairies being sighted on both of these roads. On one of the fairy roads an old resident claimed to have witnessed an entire regiment of fairy soldiers returning from

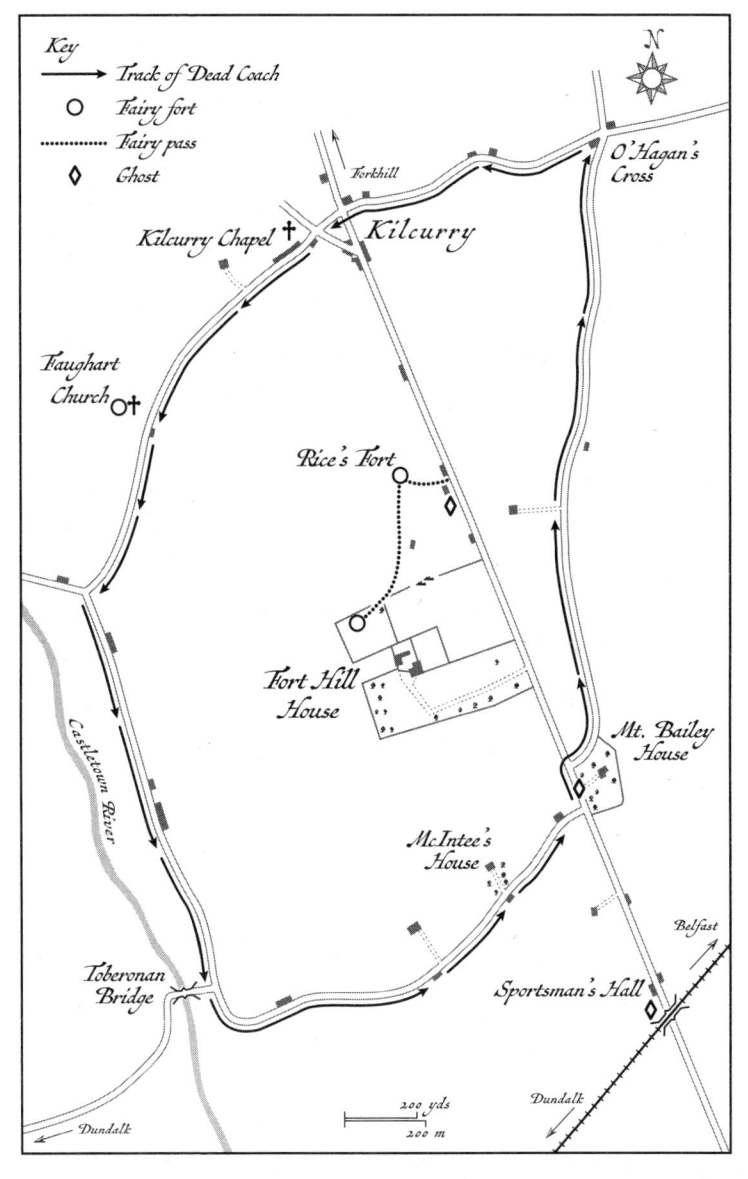

Map 2. The supernatural countryside around Kilcurry, County Louth, in 1899: three fairy forts, two fairy passes, three places where ghosts appeared and the route of the 'Dead Coach' that circles Kilcurry.

a campaign; and on the other one a farmworker once heard a large number of horses galloping past. A female resident of Kilcurry additionally reported that her mother had always maintained that she had once been abducted by the local fairies. Out walking one night, she had seen a woman sitting beside the river, lamenting and beating the water with her hands. She had gone over to see what the matter was, but had been seized and dragged away to one of the fairies' homes, where she remained for several days. There she was unshakable in her refusal to eat or drink anything. She begged to be allowed to return home to her children, so the fairies were finally forced to let her go. In another tale, a day labourer who lived a few miles away was abducted by fairies and spent a night on the summit of the Hill of Faughart before being taken back to his front door the following morning. The man in question used this episode to explain why he had arrived late for work on the morning in question.

In addition to this group of places with fairy associations, there were another three sites on the main road to the south of Kilcurry in the direction of Dundalk that were said to be haunted. At one of them, the ghost of a black dog was seen. At the second, the ghost of a former inhabitant of the house at Mount Bailey was seen walking along the road. And at the third, the ghost of a dead farmer was locked in a boarded-up cottage, while his son, who had taken over the farm on his father's death, lived in a new farmhouse with his family. And whenever any of the inhabitants of the local parish was about to die, a silent hearse was seen driving round Kilcurry along a never-changing route.

In nineteenth-century Ireland, the Good People were an integral part of a tradition inextricably bound up with the land, their legends and folktales being no less inseparable from that land. Just as was the case in Iceland, so the fairy stories of rural Ireland were often local legends about events that were said to have taken place in very specific locations within a familiar, everyday setting, in which the events in question were said to have affected people from the storyteller's own circle of acquaintances. The way in which these stories were presented in most collections of tales makes it easy to forget these topographical associations, since the anthologies were normally ordered not along geographical lines, but thematically. And yet the actual setting was of central importance for the way in which these traditions were shared by the people involved. Indeed, this is arguably the principal characteristic linking the fairy stories of rural Iceland with those of rural Ireland. In both traditions, stories were told about everyday rural life. Elves and fairies were an essential part of the world of supernatural beings that populated the land, and they contributed to providing an explanation for the blows of fate that threatened every person living in the countryside. When the tales of elves and fairies moved away from their true home in the countryside and abandoned the rural population that worked the land, an immediate change is observable. In the following chapters we shall see how elves and fairies left their rural homes and how today they have once again become linked to the land, albeit only with an abstract version of that land.

Elves and Fairies at Court

CHAPTER 3

FROM THE COUNTRYSIDE TO THE COURT

Fairies and Knights

Even during the Middle Ages there had already been an attempt to separate elves and fairies from their rural environment in one part of the narrative tradition. Not even in the Middle Ages was every section of society bound up equally closely with the land: whereas country folk often spent their whole lives on a narrowly circumscribed parcel of land and rarely left it, the lives of the aristocracy were characterized by extensive and even international networks of contacts. Itinerant singers and poets who travelled from court to court were likewise free to roam far and wide, as they were not tied down to any one place. In extreme cases, the lives of the members of this social grouping might unfold on a stage that extended to practically the whole of Europe, so that – in addition to local tales – they cultivated a kind of literature that was just as international in its geographical range as the social networks of the leading aristocratic families.

The most important example of this development is to be found in the world of legends surrounding King Arthur and his knights of the Round Table. Few other stories were as popular throughout practically the whole of Europe as the cycle of Arthurian legends, in which elves and fairies played a central role; and yet the pan-European popularity of these tales also means that large parts of this literature were not tied to any one place. Although there were areas throughout Europe with Arthurian associations, events that can occur anywhere ultimately take place nowhere: in the final analysis, the land of international Arthurian literature was a fantasy land from a bygone age associated with great feats of knightly valour. The elves and fairies that often played a central role in this literature were divorced from any actual country in these medieval narratives and despatched to some abstract 'otherworld'.

The Fairy Isle of Avalon and Related Otherworlds

The figure of King Arthur was central to a large number of poems and narratives to which he gave his name. They date from the period between 1100 and the end of the Middle Ages, and were written not only in Latin but also in every major vernacular. Their basic framework was provided by Arthur's life, whose outlines were initially established in the first half of the twelfth century. It was in around 1136 that the British historian Geoffrey of Monmouth completed his *Historia Regum Britanniae* (*History of the Kings of Britain*), a work that offers the first complete account of Arthur's life. Even here, the mythical Arthur's worldly existence ends not with his death, but with him vanishing into the otherworld: he is fatally wounded in the Battle of Camlann, but he does not die from his wounds. Instead, he is taken to the Isle of Avalon to be healed, only he is never seen again in the world of mortals.

The Isle of Avalon is the most important place in the otherworld of Arthurian legend. It is mentioned only briefly in the *History of the Kings of Britain*, but within just a few years it reappears in a long poem, the *Vita Merlini* (*Life of Merlin*), that Geoffrey of Monmouth wrote in Latin between 1148 and 1155 and that contains one of the earliest and most detailed descriptions of Avalon. Here Avalon is the 'Island of Apples', and it produces everything needed in life without any need for work. Here grow a large number of apple trees. The islanders live far longer than humans normally do, and they are ruled by nine sisters. These rulers are very beautiful and also very learned: they know all about medicine, astrology and magic. The foremost of these women is Morgen, and it is she who welcomes the fatally wounded Arthur to Avalon and promises to heal him.

This Morgen is the self-same Morgain la Fée, who plays a leading role in the English and French Arthurian literature of the Middle Ages – a role that she continues to fill in modern adaptations of the material. In Geoffrey's *Life of Merlin* she is depicted in entirely positive colours, as a wise ruler and a great healer. Only later was she to be portrayed in a more ambivalent manner and often in emphatically negative terms. And yet even in later retellings of the legend of Arthur she remains the figure who spirits the king away to Avalon at the end of his life, in the process representing one of the best-known types of female figures from the otherworld in medieval literature: the powerful fairy woman who brings human heroes back with her to the otherworld.

This type of narrative appears to be deeply rooted in the various Celtic traditions; and its widespread dissemination, which it achieved through Arthurian literature, is an important example of the profound influence of Celtic culture on that of Europe in general. In the previous chapter I discussed the Old Irish tales of *Connle's Journey to the Otherworld* and *Bran's Sea Voyage*, both of which share their principal motifs with the tales of Arthur, Avalon and Morgain la Fée. The Irish texts tell how a powerful woman from the otherworld – a *fée* in the Arthurian tradition – uses either a miraculous apple or a branch of an apple tree to lure the son of a royal Irish house to her home beyond the ocean, a place from where the human hero will never return, but where he will enjoy a life of immortality. This narrative finds an exact counterpart in the story of the disappearance of King Arthur, with the British king being taken to an Island of Apples that is ruled by a powerful sorceress – Morgain la Fée – and where life triumphs over death, so his fatal wounds can be healed here.

This type of narrative and its basic structure are found again and again in some of the most famous poems of the European Middle Ages. One of them is the *Lai de Lanval* by Marie de France that dates from the second half of the twelfth century. Practically nothing is known about the life and precise identity of the poet – only that the Old French tradition ascribes ten narrative poems, or *lais*, to her, all of them among the high points of Old French literature.

The *Lai de Lanval* is an account of its hero's journey to the otherworld. Lanval is a knight at the court of King Arthur, but whereas all Arthur's other knights are granted lands, Lanval is overlooked and goes away empty-handed. He is a prince with his own fortune, but since he is always giving it away, he ends up impoverished and is reduced to a state of despair. Broken by his grief, he rides into a forest one day, lies down beneath a tree and is overcome by self-pity. Suddenly, two beautiful, richly dressed women appear and tell Lanval that their mistress has sent them to take him to her tent, which is not far away in the forest. Lanval follows the women and soon arrives at a tent so magnificent that not even Queen Semiramis or Emperor Augustus could afford its like. Here he meets the mistress of the two ladies, a young woman of overwhelming beauty who lies half-naked on her bed in the heat of a summer's day.

The young mistress, whose name is not mentioned in the poem, tells Lanval that she has left her own realm to confess her love for him. For his part, Lanval immediately falls in love with her. She invites the knight into her bed and promises that from now on he will always have enough wealth, no matter how open-handed he may be – generosity is an important courtly virtue. She imposes only one condition on him: he may tell no one of their encounter. In return, she will give him all the wealth that he needs and meet him in secret whenever he wants to see her. She will then be at his bidding.

From now on, Lanval has a vast and inexhaustible fortune at his disposal, allowing him to do good through his generosity and to acquire a respectable position at court. As a result, he comes to the attention of Arthur's wife, Queen Guinevere, who invites him to become her lover. Lanval indignantly turns her down and the situation escalates. In response to his rejection, Guinevere accuses him of being interested only in young men, prompting Lanval to taunt her by saying that he is in a liaison with a woman and that even the woman's servants are more beautiful than Queen Guinevere. Guinevere is so mortified that she tells Arthur that Lanval has tried to seduce her and that he has humiliated her by claiming that his mistress's maidservants are more beautiful than the queen. Arthur is furious and decides to call Lanval to account.

But Lanval has discovered that his otherworld mistress vanished as soon as her existence was revealed. And so he is utterly devastated, even before he is summoned to appear before the king to answer for his crime of insulting the queen. Lanval is enjoined to prove that he does indeed have a lover more beautiful than Guinevere, otherwise he will have to bear the consequences of his insult. But this is something that Lanval is unable to do, because, by revealing his lover's existence, he has violated the rule that she imposed on him and in this way he has lost her for ever.

Lanval is set a deadline to prove that his claims are true. On the very last day before it expires, some wondrously beautiful women arrive at Arthur's court on horseback. Although only servants, they are fairer than the queen. When their mistress finally appears on a white stallion, the poet states that she is more beautiful than the whole world. In the face of such beauty, Arthur is obliged to acquit Lanval: his mistress and even her maidservants are fairer than the queen. But nothing can persuade this woman to remain at Arthur's court, and when she turns her horse around and prepares to leave, Lanval leaps up behind her and rides away to Avalon with her. He has never been heard of again.

The basic plot of the *Lai de Lanval* was so successful that the anonymous Old French *Lai de Graelent* has almost exactly the same storyline. For the edification of audiences outside the French-speaking world, it was translated into Old Norse as *Januals ljóð*, while in England we find numerous versions of the tale, including a *Sir Landevale*, a *Sir Launfal* and a *Sir Lambewell*. At the same time, however, the *Lai de Lanval* points us back to the subject's Celtic roots. As in the Irish versions of this story, a woman from the otherworld chooses a hero as her lover and at the end spirits him away for ever to her otherworldly Island of Apples, in this case Avalon. Marie de France also draws an explicit link with the Celtic world both at the beginning and at the end of her poem, as she states very clearly that it is based on a Breton tale.

The Breton *lais*, as they are called, constitute an entire genre in Old French literature: they are narrative poems written in

Old French, but drawing their plots from Breton themes. In this particular instance, the term 'Breton' is ambiguous, as the corresponding French word can refer both to the Celtic-speaking inhabitants of Brittany and to British Arthurian literature. It is an ambiguity due to the fact that Brittany was settled in late antiquity and in the early Middle Ages by new arrivals from Great Britain. Historically speaking, Brittany was 'Little' Britain, in contradistinction to 'Great' Britain. In other words, 'Breton *lais*' are ostensibly or genuinely French reworkings of Breton or British poems; but what matters most here is that in both cases they are based on Celtic material.

As a result, there is a certain thematic unity to the poems. A number of anonymous *lais* have survived alongside those of Marie de France. Among them is a *Lai de Guingamor* about a Breton knight who sets off in pursuit of a white boar that every previous knight has failed to bring down. This hunt takes Guingamor deep into the forest, where he fords a dangerous river and reaches a large castle surrounded by walls of green marble and studded with precious gemstones. Surprised, he breaks off his hunt in order to explore the unbelievably magnificent building, which appears to be completely empty. Utterly amazed, he looks all round it and then resumes his hunt. But by now he has almost lost all trace of the white boar.

After a while, Guingamor hears his hunting dog barking and follows it to a spring at the foot of an olive tree that is in blossom. On the bed of the spring are pebbles of gold and silver, and in it a naked young woman is bathing. She is fairer than any other in the whole wide world. She and the knight strike up a conversation and it is not long before they are a couple. The nameless woman promises to hand over the white boar in three days' time and to let Guingamor return to his own country. They spend the intervening time at her castle, which is the same one that Guingamor had earlier found empty. But now there are three hundred knights there, accompanied by a bevy of beautiful women. Guingamor spends the next two days at the castle, where he is entertained with music and a series of banquets. On the third day, he plans to return home with the white boar, and his lover does indeed hand the animal over. But at the same time she warns him that nothing will be gained by his riding back to court, because he has spent three hundred years in the castle, and his king and all of his friends and kinsfolk have long since died. Guingamor refuses to believe her and insists on riding home. The woman allows him to leave, but dismisses him with a warning: once he has forded the river that divides their two lands, he may not eat or drink anything until he is back at her side.

Guingamor sets off back across the river in his boat; but when he reaches the other side, he sees that the forest has changed out of all recognition. He meets a charcoal burner and asks him the way. The charcoal burner replies that the king has been dead for three hundred years, while Guingamor himself is the subject of a legend that tells how he disappeared one day while out hunting. Guingamor tells the charcoal burner the rest of his story, then retraces his steps with the aim of returning to the woman's castle.

On his way there he starts to feel hungry, and sees an apple tree growing beside the path. He picks three of the ripest and juiciest apples and eats them, at which point he immediately grows so old and so weak that he falls from his horse and can no longer stand. He is lying on the ground when two women arrive and reproach him for his actions. But they then help him to his feet and accompany him back across the river.

This poem, too, follows the same basic pattern as the *Lai de Lanval* and the other narratives that we have already examined. Since the mistress of the otherworldly castle has power over the white boar, we can assume that she sent it to lure

Guingamor to her. In short, this poem, too, reflects the same basic structure of a female figure from the otherworld engineering a meeting with a knight and making him her lover. After a brief return to the land of mortals, the knight is spirited away to the otherworld for good. The *Lai de Guingamor* adds a further motif in the form of the otherworld's completely different way of measuring time. In the case of Ireland, we have already encountered these themes in the *Lay of Oisín in the Land of the Young*, where the hero returns from a world whose inhabitants never age and makes the mistake of breaking the injunction that has been placed on him, with the result that he suddenly ages by several centuries. In the *Lai de Guingamor*, it is apples that lead to the knight's downfall – a motif that recalls the apples and apple trees in *Connle's Journey to the Otherworld*, *Bran's Sea Voyage* and the Island of Apples that is Avalon. In other words, all these stories about the otherworld are constructed from very similar motifs that appear to derive directly or indirectly from the Celtic world, and perhaps specifically from Ireland.

The supernatural and powerful female figures of these narratives about the otherworld are all examples of the *fée* (or fairy), as she is called in French. In the Middle Ages, we encounter these figures first and foremost in texts written by members of the highest stratum in society – namely, the aristocracy – with the result that within this framework it is knights and kings, not members of the impoverished lower orders and of the rural community, who interact with these figures. There is only sporadic evidence in the surviving sources of these fairies being figures of popular belief in addition to their literary existence. In other words, they are rarely a part of the world of ideas of the less-privileged classes in society, and play almost no practical role in that world. The most significant exception is found in the case records of the trial for heresy of Joan of Arc (born *c.* 1412), the 'Maid of Orléans'. During the Hundred Years' War between France and England, Joan led the French army to a significant victory at Orléans but was later captured by pro-English fighters, hauled before the authorities and burnt at the stake as a heretic in 1431.

The detailed records of the trial contain rare evidence of the popular belief in fairies at this time. It is said that there was a tree outside Joan's home village of Domrémy that was known variously as the 'Ladies' Tree' and the 'Fairies' Tree', or the 'arbre charmine faée de Bourlémont' (the enchanted fairy tree of Bourlémont). Near this tree was a spring that was visited by people suffering from a fever, who would drink from its waters. Others who were sick would also walk round it in a circle. Some of the region's elderly population reported that the tree was visited by fairies, and some even claimed to have seen them themselves. Joan admitted that, together with a number of other young girls from the village, she had sometimes made garlands for Our Lady of Domrémy and placed them in the branches of this tree. She also stated that she had heard rumours that people had gone to the tree specifically to see the fairies; but Joan insisted that she did not believe this and regarded it all as witchcraft.

This image of the tree and the spring recalls the scene in the *Lai de Guingamor* when the knight meets the nameless fairy, while the latter is bathing beneath the tree. But unlike the spring in the poem, the one at Domrémy was intended to be used only by simple country folk and to address their everyday concerns relating to illness and to their recovery from the same. While the *lai* was about chivalric adventures, the cult of the spring at Domrémy was all about dealing with the harshness of daily life without any medical care. For the author of a courtly poem on the one hand, and for the population of a rural community on the other, places such as a fairy tree and a fairy spring meant very different things. They may not have belonged to two different worlds, each of which was hermetically sealed from the other, but they reflected different perspectives on a view of the world that in many respects was shared by the aristocracy and by the poor, in spite of the conflicts between them: people could adapt that view to suit their varying needs.

That logic was not always involved here is especially well illustrated by one particular detail, when Joan admitted that she and a number of other young women had made garlands for Our Lady of Domrémy – the Virgin Mary – and hung them in the fairy tree. How clear was it, in fact, whether these garlands in the fairy tree were intended for the fairy who lived in the spring, or dedicated to the Mother of God? Did anyone ask for which of these otherworldly figures they were meant and how anyone was expected to distinguish between them? The veneration of fairies and the cult of the saint seem to have merged seamlessly with each other in Domrémy. For the aristocratic judges who made up the inquisition, this was proof of heresy and witchcraft; but for the local population, it was a way of dealing with the harsh realities of everyday life.

Echoes of the Hero Who Has Been Spirited Away: Thomas the Rhymer and Tam Lin

The fairies who feature in Old French literature and the ones that were venerated in Domrémy are powerful women with the ability to rule the lives of kings and commoners alike: figures whose position on a local level might even come close to that of the Virgin. The tales that are told about them in Arthurian romance and in the Breton *lais* often revolve around the motif of a male hero or knight being spirited away to an otherworld, where he becomes the lover – or plaything? – of a woman from the otherworld.

Both parts of this motif – the fairy as a powerful female figure and the spiriting away of the hero – continue to resonate in the reception of these tales right down to the present day. And yet there is one motif that is missing entirely from the versions of the narrative that have just been summarized and that was later to become so important: that of the fairy queen. The fairies of the Old French literary tradition are extremely powerful, but they do not have a royal title. The now widespread idea that fairies live in a kingdom ruled by a king or a queen is first found at a relatively late date and in a different part of Europe. Two of the most influential examples of this shift combine the idea of a fairy queen with the basic outlines of the fairy stories of the Arthurian world and of the Breton *lais*: namely, the Scottish tales of Thomas the Rhymer and Tam Lin.

Thomas the Rhymer and Tam Lin are the heroes – or antiheroes – of Scottish tales that scholars such as Diane Purkiss have interpreted as the direct descendants of medieval tales about fairies.[1] Both are known chiefly from later ballads from southern Scotland that were probably not written down until the seventeenth or eighteenth centuries, but which were to exert a marked influence on depictions of fairies in literature and music in the twentieth and twenty-first centuries.

Thomas the Rhymer – or Thomas of Erceldoune – was actually a thirteenth-century Scottish poet. Practically nothing is known about him, although by the early fourteenth century he already enjoyed a reputation of having been a seer and a prophet. By the early fifteenth century, a collection of prophecies, all of which were attributed to him, had appeared under the title *The Romance and Prophecies of Thomas of Erceldoune*. The narrative poem *Thomas of Erceldoune*, which dates from sometime between 1401 and 1430, ascribes his gift of prophecy to the queen of the fairies: having gained the favour of the queen of Elfland, Thomas lives in her realm for three (or according to other versions, seven) years, which seem to him to be no more than three (or seven) days. But the time comes for Elfland to pay its dues to Hell. The queen is afraid that the Devil will choose Thomas as his tribute, and so she sends him back to the world of humans in an attempt to protect him. Thomas asks for a memento to show that he has spoken to her, which is when she gives him the gift of prophecy.

In the early eighteenth century, the tale of Thomas of Erceldoune inspired a ballad that was hugely popular and that has come down to us in several versions. The action takes place at Eildon Hill in the Scottish Borders. The most famous version begins with Thomas seeing a woman dressed in green silk riding past the Eildon Tree. He sinks to his knees at the sight of her and addresses her as the queen of Heaven. Although there is an echo here of the Virgin Mary at Domrémy, there is undoubtedly also an ironic undertone in the present ballad. Here, too, the boundaries between the woman from the otherworld and the Mother of God are blurred. Yet the rider sets him straight: she is not the queen of Heaven, but the queen of Elfland, and she has come to visit Thomas. She challenges him to kiss her lips, but explains that if he does so, his body will be hers. Undeterred, Thomas kisses her beneath the Eildon Tree. The queen now tells him that he has to spend seven years with her and, lifting him onto her milk-white steed, she rides away with him. After they have been riding for a very long time, they come to a garden, where the fairy queen plucks an apple from a tree and gives it to Thomas as his reward, adding that it will give him a tongue that can never lie. Thomas protests that this means he will never again be able to sell or buy anything at any market; never again be in a position to speak to a prince or a nobleman;

and never again be able to sue for a woman's favours. The queen's answer is simple: Thomas should say nothing, but just do her bidding as this is how it must be. For the next seven years, Thomas is not seen in the land of mortals.

Unlike the heroes of the Breton *lais*, Thomas returns to the world of men after spending seven years in Elfland. This return is also the central theme of another influential ballad from the Scottish Borders: the *Ballad of Tam Lin*. The earliest references to the story of Tam Lin can be traced back to the sixteenth century, although the nine or so surviving versions of the ballad must have been written at a much later date. Some of these versions reveal striking differences, but all begin with a warning to young women to stay away from Carterhaugh, because this is where 'young Tam Lin' is to be found, and no woman goes to Carterhaugh without leaving something behind, be it a ring, a fine cloak or her virginity. The young and beautiful Janet – in some versions she is called Lady Margaret – is a daughter of the nobility. Despite all the warnings, she goes to Carterhaugh to pick roses. Tam Lin immediately appears and bids her give an account of herself. The two become involved in an argument over who has the rightful claim to the roses of Carterhaugh. Tam Lin then has sex with her – and from this point onwards, most versions of the ballad describe him as her one true love and as 'the man she loves the most'.

But their liaison does not last, and after they have made love Janet/Lady Margaret looks round for Tam Lin, only to find he has disappeared. It is as if he has vanished into thin air. And so she returns to her father's court. Eight months later it is plain for all to see that she is expecting a child. She refuses to reveal the father's identity, but returns to Carterhaugh to pick some plants designed to induce a miscarriage. As soon as she starts to pick them, Tam Lin reappears. Janet/Lady Margaret complains that her lover is not human and cannot be the father of her child. Only now does Tam Lin explain that he is not an elf, but a baptized Christian and the oldest son and heir of a great noble family. As a child, he had fallen asleep beneath an apple tree and had been abducted by the queen of Elfland. He describes Elfland as a delightful place, but one that every ten years has to pay a tithe to Hell – and Tam Lin is afraid that he will be the next offering. So he tells Janet/Lady Margaret how he can be taken back to the world of humans. At Halloween, the entire elfin court rides out and roams the world with the king and queen at its head, and with Tam Lin riding on a milk-white horse among the knights that bring up the rear of the procession. At an agreed place, Janet/Lady Margaret would have an opportunity to catch him and drag him from his horse. Once he has been captured, the fairy queen will transform him into an entire kaleidoscope of different shapes, but if Janet/Lady Margaret can hold him tight until the following morning, he will be free and will belong to her for good. Janet/Lady Margaret does as she is told and goes to the place that the elves will ride past. At the very end of the procession she sees Tam Lin and grabs him. The fairy queen turns him successively into fire, iron, various animals and a silk thread, but Janet/Lady Margaret refuses to let go, and the next morning she finds herself holding a naked man in her arms. She takes him home to her father's court and the news of her feat spreads to the whole of Scotland.

These tales about Scottish aristocrats draw on motifs very similar to the ones found in the older Arthurian legends and the Breton *lais*. All of them are products of an aristocratic world of knights and royal courts, a world that was dominated by men and by ideals of manliness. Despite this, men's images of themselves are systematically undermined here: the knights and 'heroes' of these tales are men who are entirely dependent on the help and grace of female figures. Arthur owes his life to the female ruler of Avalon; the knight Lanval allows himself to be supported by his otherworld lover and owes her both his material affluence and his ability to escape from courtly intrigues; the knight Guingamor becomes the plaything of a fairy, who fulfils his every desire but who ultimately takes everything from him; Thomas the Rhymer is entirely in thrall to the power of the fairy queen and owes her his gift of prophecy, a gift that will make him immortal; and Tam Lin, too, is the fairy queen's plaything and can escape from her power not by his own strength alone, but with the help of a mortal woman. In short, fairyland is a land of subversion, an otherworld in which the male superiority of the warrior and nobleman is undermined by the fact that he repeatedly has to be rescued by a woman.

And yet, no matter how much the ideals of manhood may be questioned in these texts, there is one thing that is never in doubt: the significance of class differences. When Janet/Lady Margaret goes to Carterhaugh to pick roses and is taken to task by Tam Lin, she counters by saying that her father gave her Carterhaugh as her inheritance. That is, she is no poor peasant girl, but – like Tam Lin himself – the heir to an estate as a member of the Scottish aristocracy: the two of them meet as equals. What happens when the common people get above themselves is illustrated by the case of Joan of Arc, who is the daughter of a peasant, and by the cult of fairies in the village of Domrémy: it all ends on the inquisitors' pyre. The world of courtly heroes and the peasant world each has its own fairies, and the fairy world of the knights is as fundamentally different from that of the peasantry as are their social worlds. The tales told by and for the aristocracy speak of the world of fairies in a way that is almost entirely removed from the everyday concerns of ordinary people. The peasant tales of rural Ireland and of rural Iceland are all about the land and the harshness of a life that is spent on that land, whereas the tales of the aristocracy deal with questions of social coexistence, and with power and prestige within a ruling elite.

CHAPTER 4

FROM THE COURT TO THE TOWN

Between *A Midsummer Night's Dream*, Witchcraft and Learned Treatises

The gulf between the images of fairies that we find among members of the ruling elite and those that existed among poorer sections of the rural population was deepening dramatically during the early modern period, in the sixteenth and seventeenth centuries. In literary works such as Edmund Spenser's *The Faerie Queene* (1590–96) and in the plays of Shakespeare, elves and fairies served to glorify the royal house and to entertain the urban population (Illus. 9). At the same time, a wave of witch trials was sweeping across Scotland, in which any contact with the fairy world was treated as a crime punishable by death. This was a time when two drastically conflicting views of these supernatural beings evolved, in the form of the creative reception of fairies in art and the brutal persecution of popular forms of religious belief among the common folk, who regarded fairies as very real. This chapter will examine these early modern tensions, with reference to examples from the history of literature and religion in England and Scotland.

THE FAERIE QVEENE.

Disposed into twelue bookes,

Fashioning

XII. Morall vertues.

LONDON
Printed for VVilliam Ponsonbie.
1596.

m. 47.

9. The title page of the 1596 printing of Spenser's *The Faerie Queene*.

There will then follow a kind of synthetic approach, with a preview of the figure of the folklorist, illustrated here by reference to the 'Fairy Minister' Robert Kirk (*c.* 1644–92).

Fairies in the Literature of the Tudor Age: Edmund Spenser and William Shakespeare

The years between 1558 and 1603, when the Tudor queen, Elizabeth I, was on the throne, witnessed the publication of a whole series of pioneering works on the fairy motif. Perhaps the most extraordinary, if not the most influential, of these was *The Faerie Queene*, a status that it owes not only to its vast length, but also to its close links with the royal house. Edmund Spenser (*c.* 1552–99) published this verse epic in two parts, in 1590 and 1596, and dedicated it to the queen. In all, it runs to more than 36,000 lines.

The Faerie Queene consists of six completed books and two that were unfinished. All of them follow the same basic model: a fairy knight – who in one instance is female – rides out in the name of his or her queen. In the course of that quest, the knight fights many battles and is subjected to many ordeals, while evolving from an uncouth, boorish individual, and acquiring and perfecting a particular virtue. Each book deals with a specific virtue: Holiness, Temperance, Chastity, Friendship, Justice and Courtesy – the last of these a reference to the perfect behaviour befitting the rank of a member of the royal court. Each book presents one of these virtues in allegorical form. Every courtier of the time was expected to demonstrate these qualities.

The work's title refers to its framing action: the fairy queen sends six of her knights out on a particular quest. The court of this fairy queen is a mirror of the Arthurian court of the medieval chivalric romances, in which King Arthur sits at his

Round Table and allows his knights to ride out in search of adventure. The picture of the fairy queen in Spenser's epoch-making poem is drawn entirely from these medieval chivalric romances, but he has transformed it in such a way that the female ruler – the fairy queen, instead of King Arthur – can be interpreted as an allegory of the contemporary Queen Elizabeth I, who laid the foundations for the moral perfection of her court and, hence, of England as a whole. On the other hand, the details of the plot remain largely unaffected by the myths and legends about elves and fairies, one of the few exceptions being a detailed account of fairy stories in the tenth canto of Book One, when a knight who is believed to be an elf discovers that he is not an elf at all, but an English prince who had been abducted by a fairy and replaced by her own 'base Elfin brood' – in other words, by a 'chaungeling' (*sic*). As a man and as a Christian, this knight can now rescue the Anglican Protestant Church in allegorical guise.

Spenser's *The Faerie Queene* shows that, in the immediate context of the cult of the ruling English royal house, myths and legends about elves and fairies could find their way into English literature shortly after the Reformation, albeit only in allegorical form and only when suitably adapted to social power structures and to the Protestant view of the world. The theatre seems to have enjoyed a somewhat greater degree of freedom, in part because it did not appeal specifically to a courtly audience, but rather to a broader cross-section of the urban population. Spenser's *The Faerie Queene* lost much of its relevance once the Tudor Age was over, whereas William Shakespeare (*c.* 1564–1616) was to propose ideas about the world of fairies in his plays, whose influence continues to reverberate right down to the present day.

A Midsummer Night's Dream dates from the mid-1590s and received a number of performances before first appearing in print in 1600, quickly establishing itself as one of Shakespeare's most popular and most widely performed works. Few other texts have exerted such an influence on the cultural history of elves and fairies. In the course of his comedy, Shakespeare introduces us to a group of figures that even today continues to provide the basis for new creative engagements with the world of elves and fairies.

The play is set in Athens in mythical Greek antiquity, at a time when the ruler is the hero Theseus. Later, the action transfers to a nearby wood frequented by fairies. Theseus is about to marry the Amazon Queen Hippolyta, when a dispute arises between an implacable father and his daughter, resulting in two tragic pairs of lovers being driven into the fairy wood. At the same time, a group of 'rude mechanicals' decides to use the wood as a place in which to rehearse the play that they will perform at their ruler's nuptials. Having entered the fairy forest, the human lovers and the actors are caught up in an argument between the king and queen of fairyland, Oberon and Titania, each of whom reproaches the other for their amorous intrigues with mortals. Among these mortals are the current rulers of Athens: Oberon accuses Titania of being in love with Theseus, while Titania claims that Oberon is Hippolyta's lover and that he has come to bless her wedding bed. The quarrel between Oberon and Titania even upsets the natural order, so that winds infect the land with a pestilence, the rivers overflow their banks and the harvest rots in the fields: the fairies' royal couple appears to represent an elemental force that decides the fertility and wellbeing of humans and land alike.

The argument gets out of hand when Oberon demands that Titania surrender the 'changeling boy', who is a member of her retinue. This changeling is the son of an Indian king, whose mother had been Titania's confidante, but who died in childbirth. Oberon now wants to make this boy his knight. When two groups of completely helpless mortals stumble upon a situation which, to put it mildly, is already fraught, and when the intruders refuse to behave in a way that Oberon thinks seemly, the king of the fairies summons his principal courtier, Robin Goodfellow, also known as Puck. Puck is a mischievous rogue who has already played many tricks on humans, stealing cream from milk, startling village women, misleading night wanderers and then laughing at them. Oberon decides to teach both Titania and the various mortals a lesson and uses Puck to this end. Puck duly initiates a series of pranks, none of which goes as planned, with the result that Oberon finally has to intervene and ensure that not only are he and Titania reconciled, but so too are the mortal lovers, allowing the play to end on a happy note. The last word is given to Puck, who, in an epilogue, invites the audience not to take offence at the shadows that they have seen and to regard these visions of the fairy realm as nothing more than dreams.

The picture of fairyland that Shakespeare conjures up in *A Midsummer Night's Dream* draws on multiple sources, and in the course of the centuries that followed proved immensely influential. One of these sources was medieval Arthurian legend, the play's depiction of a fairy world ruled by a king and queen ultimately deriving from the accounts of elves and fairies found in Arthurian literature, as by the late Middle Ages the aristocratic focus of these tales had led to the establishment of the idea of an actual fairy *kingdom* – I earlier mentioned the fifteenth-century poem *Thomas of Erceldoune*. It was precisely at the time of *A Midsummer Night's Dream* that this idea of a fairy kingdom found arguably its most monumental expression in Spenser's *The Faerie Queene*.

The names of the fairy king and queen can be traced back to rather different roots. The figure of the powerful fairy king Oberon derives from the Old French chivalric romance *Huon de Bordeaux*, which was set down in writing shortly after 1260. This anonymous poem introduces us to the figure of Auberon, who is portrayed as a mighty sorcerer and the ruler of a sylvan kingdom. At his birth, supernatural beings had invested him with great power; but at the same time they had placed a curse on him, with the result that Auberon remained markedly small of stature. By the middle of the fifteenth century, he was appearing in the records of English trials as a creature from the spirit world called Oberion. As such, he was routinely invoked by magicians performing their rituals. It was only a small step from here to Shakespeare's use of the name for a more or less benevolent king of the fairies with the power to do magic.

The figure of Robin Goodfellow is first found in British texts about elves in 1489 and is mentioned several times in the course of the following decades, before Shakespeare gave this name to one of his principal protagonists and equated him with Puck. By the 1590s, the figure of Puck was already several centuries old: Anglo-Saxon texts of the early Middle Ages mention him as a spirit who leads travellers astray at night, just as Shakespeare says about Puck. In *A Midsummer Night's Dream*, Shakespeare merged the traditional figure of Puck with the younger Robin Goodfellow, in the process turning him into one of the most prominent figures within the fairy realm.

Shakespeare's figures of Oberon and Puck reveal certain affinities with the fairy traditions of the time, whereas the name of Titania for the queen of the fairies is largely Shakespeare's own invention. This name does not derive from any British fairy tradition, but from the literature of classical antiquity: in Ovid's *Metamorphoses*, Titania is one of the names by which the Roman goddess of the hunt was known. As such, she was the mistress of forests and woodland. Ovid's

Metamorphoses was well known to educated audiences in Shakespeare's day, so the allusion would have been understood by many theatregoers. This choice of name evoked associations of divine dignity and of the prestige of ancient Rome. One possible motivation here may have been the fact that Elizabeth I was still on the English throne when Shakespeare's play was first performed and published. After Spenser had drawn a stylized portrait of the last Tudor monarch in *The Faerie Queene*, the queen of the fairies in *A Midsummer Night's Dream* was also to be a figure of comparable regal dignity.

The enhanced status accorded to the queen of the fairies in *A Midsummer Night's Dream* may also have served to set her apart from another description of a not dissimilar figure whom Shakespeare introduced into his tragedy *Romeo and Juliet*, which was first published in 1597. Here Queen Mab makes a brief appearance. Described as 'the fairies' midwife', she rides over the faces of sleepers in her tiny carriage and helps to give birth to their desires in the form of dreams. Mercutio describes her in Act One Scene Four:

> She is the fairies' midwife, and she comes
> In shape no bigger than an agate stone
> On the forefinger of an alderman,
> Drawn with a team of little atomi
> Athwart men's noses as they lie asleep.
> Her wagon spokes made of long spinners' legs;
> The cover, of the wings of grasshoppers;
> Her traces, of the moonshine's wat'ry beams;
> Her collars, of the smallest spider web;
> Her whip, of cricket's bone, the lash of film;
> Her wagoner, a small grey-coated gnat
> Not half so big as a round little worm
> Pricked from the lazy finger of a maid.

> Her chariot is an empty hazelnut
> Made by the joiner squirrel or old grub,
> Time out o' mind the fairies' coachmakers.
> And in this state she gallops night by night
> Through lovers' brains, and then they dream of love.[1]

Here the fairy queen is a tiny creature who belongs entirely to the world of dreams over which she holds sway. The idea of tiny fairies also resonates in *A Midsummer Night's Dream*, where we discover at one point that the argument between Oberon and Titania has so terrified the fairies that they have hidden in oak apples. These fairies are as small as Mab, whose carriage is made from a hazelnut. In general, however, the fairies in *A Midsummer Night's Dream* are the same size as humans, a substantial part of the play involving Titania falling in love with Bottom the Weaver under the influence of a magic potion. He, too, has had a spell cast upon him, but has manifestly not shrunk in size.

The picture of the fairy court that Shakespeare paints in *A Midsummer Night's Dream* draws on several different traditions: motifs from folklore and popular belief (Puck); medieval chivalric romances and contemporary practices in the field of magic (Oberon); and the sort of material that is associated with a classical education (Titania). Taking these as his starting point, Shakespeare went on to create a new picture of a magical otherworld that not only exudes a great sense of dignity, but also incorporates elements of the burlesque. In the form in which it appears in *A Midsummer Night's Dream*, Shakespeare's world of fairies is one that he himself has created, and yet it was this very form that was to prove so immensely successful. Henry Purcell adapted the play for his semi-opera *The Fairy-Queen* of 1692; it inspired Mendelssohn's Overture of 1826 and Britten's opera of 1960; and Carl Orff spent many years from 1917 to 1962 working on a setting. No less pervasive was the play's impact on painting and literature. Nor was it only in the English-speaking world that the post-Shakespearean artistic and literary reception of the fairy realm was largely influenced by attempts to engage with Shakespeare's own view of it.

Outside the fields of art and literature, however, responses to the world of elves and fairies were by no means as unproblematic as the success of Shakespeare's adaptation might suggest. Indeed, even Shakespeare's own version reflects contemporary tensions: at the end of the final act, Puck is required to speak an epilogue in which he expresses his hope that he has not offended his audience, and he concludes by explaining that the play is no more than an innocent dream. Such an epilogue may have been necessary, because not everyone at this time regarded the fairy kingdom as a world of dreams that existed only in the imagination.

King James I and the Fairies of the Scottish Witch Trials

Following her death, Elizabeth was succeeded by James I. He had been born in Edinburgh in 1566 and, as James VI, had become king of Scotland the following year. Elizabeth died childless, and so on her death in 1603 James ascended the English throne as the great-grandson of James IV's English wife, Margaret Tudor. Between 1603 and his death in 1625, he was king of both Scotland and England. He is remembered today as the prime mover behind the most important English translation of the Bible, a project in which he was closely involved and that came to fruition in 1611, with the publication of the King James Bible. In terms of the politics of religion, however, the Protestant James was influential not only through his translation of the Bible: during his years as king of Scotland he also portrayed himself to the world as Satan's greatest foe on earth, by championing a universal reform of the Church and, more especially, by seeking to thwart the Devil's influence through a series of witch trials. This, at least, was how he himself saw things.

The king's interest in witchcraft found its first official expression in the wake of a particularly stormy sea voyage that inspired him with the delusional idea that the tempest was the work of witches plotting to end his life. This led to the witch trial of North Berwick that was held in Edinburgh in 1590/91 under the personal supervision of the king, allowing James to present himself as the defender of the Protestant faith against all who had sealed a pact with Satan.

His first detailed account of his view of witchcraft – and an outstanding example of the ability to spread panic as part of a propaganda campaign on the part of the crown – was his treatise *Daemonologie*, which was published in Edinburgh in 1597 and repeatedly reprinted during the years that followed, when it was also translated into multiple other languages (Illus. 10). Here James developed his theory of witchcraft, which interpreted every kind of magical practice and every encounter with supernatural beings as the work of the Devil. In turn, this had important implications for his contemporaries' view of elves and fairies. In traditional popular belief, these beings had occupied an unclear intermediary position in an ill-defined grey area between the world of God and of the good and that of the Devil and of evil. In this context, there is evidence that elves and fairies were interpreted as angels that had remained neutral at the time of Lucifer's revolt against God. But James's *Daemonologie* and the ideology underpinning the witch trials that continued in Scotland until the early eighteenth century excluded each and every grey area: all that was not God's was the Devil's.

DÆMONOLOGIE, IN FORME OF A DIA-LOGVE,

Diuided into three books:

WRITTEN BY THE HIGH and mightie Prince, IAMES by the grace of God King of England, Scotland, France and Ireland, Defender of the Faith, &c.

LONDON,
Printed by *Arnold Hatfield* for
Robert Wald-graue.
1603

10. The title page of the *Daemonologie* of King James I.

In the fifth chapter of his Third Book, James expounded his opinion on contemporary conceptions of fairies. In his view, fairies ('Phairie') or 'our good neighboures' were 'one of the sortes of illusiones that was rifest in the time of *Papistrie*'.[2] As key elements in his contemporaries' ideas about fairies, King James includes stories about a king and queen of fairyland and their carefree court, who were entitled to a share of all human goods, who abducted humans and who could offer them gifts. James himself asked a legitimate question in his treatise: how could it be that witches went to their deaths after confessing that a fairy had taken them to a mound that had opened up to receive them, and that on entering it they had encountered a beautiful queen who, a figure of light, had given them a stone having many wondrous properties? To this question, too, James had an answer: these people had been tricked by the Devil. Although they did indeed believe that they had visited the fairy queen's court, this visit was in fact no more than a diabolical illusion. In practice, this meant that everyone who referred to the fairy world was placed on a par with Devil-worshippers and must be punished with the appropriate rigour.

James's *Daemonologie* is a particularly striking example of a more general trend in the years between 1560 and 1700, representing, as it does, an ever-widening gulf between the world of ideas of the 'simple people' and the convictions of the secular and ecclesiastical elite. This gulf existed not just in theory, but also in the specific practices associated with the exercise of power. Between around 1590 and 1661/62 Scotland experienced several waves of witch hunts, accompanied by a significant number of trials and an estimated 1,500 executions. The records of many of these trials have survived, and at least 113 of them refer specifically to elves and fairies.

One example is the trial of Stein Maltman, who in 1628 was accused of sorcery and witchcraft in Stirling. The case was, for the most part, not about any harm that Maltman might have done to others, as most of the acts of magic that he was accused of perpetrating had, in fact, served to heal the sick. But healing people by magic was also regarded by the authorities as witchcraft. In Maltman's case, an aggravating factor was his claim that he had learnt his healing practices from the 'fairye folk'. As a result, his supernatural healing powers stemmed from the source that James I, in his *Daemonologie*, had identified as an illusion of satanic origin. The trial records also contain one of the details that is described in the *Daemonologie* as typical of contemporary practices in the field of magic: namely, that the fairies gave magic stones to the humans with whom they came into contact. In his testimony, Maltman called one such stone an 'Elff arrow stone' – presumably a Stone Age arrowhead. He repeatedly described these stones as a cure for ailments, including the 'fairies schott', which may have been a form of lumbago (German has a similar word – *Hexenschuss*, literally 'witches' shot' – for the same ailment).

Despite the king's rabble-rousing propaganda and his attempt to equate fairies with demonic forces, the Devil is not mentioned at all in the court documents relating to Stein Maltman's trial. If we may believe these records, the trial involved no torture, and the clerks who recorded his testimony simply wrote down verbatim the comments made by this traditional healer – comments that he expressed on the strength of a belief system grounded in the folk. In short, his testimony was largely untouched by the ideas that were held by the authorities and by contemporary theologians. The fact that this was by no means always the case is well illustrated a generation later by the records of one of the most famous of all Scottish witch trials, which was held in 1662, during the last of the major Scottish witch hunts. This was the trial of Isobel Gowdie.

In four detailed confessions, Isobel Gowdie laid bare a whole range of diabolical involvements. According to the court records, she made these confessions without any recourse to torture; but since torture was always an implicit threat in the background, her 'confessions' may well have been an attempt on the part of a terrified victim to tell her judges what they wanted to hear. A generation earlier, the Devil had played no part in Stein Maltman's admission, but he was now an omnipresent force. Time and again, Gowdie confessed in detail how she had renounced her holy baptism and been rebaptized by the Devil in person. She claimed to have been one of thirteen members of a coven that worshipped the Devil with orgies, during which he consorted sexually with the women. This pact with the Devil gave these women magical abilities in the areas of food and health – that is, two everyday concerns of the poorer members of society. In this way, the Devil taught the members of the coven a Catholic (!) prayer designed to cure various kinds of fever; ways of healing sick children; incantations aimed at obtaining a good price for one's products at the market; ways of appropriating some of the produce belonging to other farmers; and ways of purloining some of the fish caught by other fishermen. On several occasions, Isobel Gowdie spoke of the fairy world: each of the thirteen members of the coven was attended by a 'sprit', that is a sprite or spirit. Several of these sprites were dressed in green, as is also the case with many descriptions of elves. One of them was called Thomas a Fearie. Downie Hill would open up for the witches, and inside they would see the queen of the fairies, beautifully dressed in white linen. Here they were served meat as part of a banquet (meat being eaten only on special occasions). They also saw the king of the fairies, who was described as a good-looking man. The fairy bulls, conversely, left Gowdie feeling afraid. Parts of her testimony consisted of an inextricable mixture of fairy mythology and ideas about the Devil: Gowdie reported that the witches received elf arrowheads from the Devil and that she was expected to shoot them at people and kill them. She admitted that her coven had killed a dozen victims in this way. As for the source of these objects, Gowdie claimed that she herself had seen them being produced: first, they were moulded by the Devil with his own hands and then sharpened by 'elf-boyes' using a special tool. Satan and the fairies had a kind of production line going, their aim being to bring about the death of innocent human beings.

In the stories that Isobel Gowdie told her judges as part of her 'confession', she had made the picture of the new fairy kingdom completely her own. This was a picture that powerful figures like James VI had foisted on the world through his *Daemonologie*: the land of the fairies had merged inextricably with that of the Devil. These developments also help to explain a curious motif in the ballads of Thomas of Erceldoune and Tam Lin discussed in the previous chapter. In both of these poems, the fairy queen has to pay a tribute to the Devil every seven years, a tribute that takes the form of a human sacrifice. During the early modern period, the ruling elite set about demonizing and ostracizing these figures from popular belief with an eagerness never seen before. In doing so, they changed our picture of fairies for good.

And yet society's desire to destroy the fairy realm was never sufficiently unified to suppress all knowledge of elves and fairies. While James VI was working on his *Daemonologie*, Shakespeare was staging *A Midsummer Night's Dream* and celebrating one of his greatest successes. Even at the height of the persecution of Scottish witches, a new interest in fairyland was emerging.

The First Signs of an Interest in Folklore: The 'Fairy Minister' Robert Kirk

Robert Kirk was born in Aberfoyle in 1644, the son of a Protestant minister. His childhood and adolescence were overshadowed by the last two major witch hunts in Scotland, in 1649 and 1661/62, and these experiences were to stay with him throughout his life: a passing reference in his most famous study makes it clear that he himself attended at least one witchcraft trial. Professionally, Kirk followed in his father's footsteps and entered the Church, spending most of his life as a minister in his home town of Aberfoyle, in the Scottish Highlands. His son, also called Robert, continued the family tradition and likewise became a Protestant minister. As chance would have it, the younger Robert was minister in Dornoch in 1727, when Janet Horne was burnt as a witch there, the last person in Scotland to suffer this fate. Robert Kirk's whole life coincided with a time marked by the demonization and brutal persecution of everything supernatural that the Church disapproved of.

It is all the more remarkable that Kirk himself came to hold a very different view of the world of ideas then held by the common people. Kirk was a minister in a Gaelic-speaking rural community. He himself spoke Gaelic and played an important role in making Protestant religious writings available to a Gaelic-speaking audience, contributing significantly to the publication of the first Gaelic Bible for use in Scotland in 1688 and preparing the first metrical translation of the Psalms into Gaelic. Today, however, he is mainly remembered for his treatise *The Secret Commonwealth*, which he completed in 1691, but which still existed only in manuscript form at the time of his death the following year. It did not appear in print until over a century later. It seems to have been intended for an educated readership in London, although it was not until 1815 that it finally reached this audience, when it was rediscovered and published by Sir Walter Scott. Long before the study of folklore emerged as a scholarly discipline, *The Secret Commonwealth* proposed a kind of folkloristic perspective on the subject. It provides its readers with a systematic description of the belief in elves and fairies – Kirk used these words, and their Gaelic equivalents, interchangeably – as it was held by the Gaelic parishioners for whose spiritual welfare he was responsible as a Protestant minister.

Kirk's picture of the popular beliefs that were held in his own particular region of Scotland mirrors what was written down much later in Gaelic Ireland in the nineteenth century, the parallels between them extending to points of detail. He tells of love affairs between female fairies and male mortals; of the abduction of infants and of women in childbirth and their replacement by changelings; of the theft of milk; of the longevity of fairies, whose thoughts are nonetheless troubled by the constant fear over whether they will be redeemed or damned on the Day of Judgement; of the fairies' fear of cold iron that can protect newborn babies in their cradles; of fairy mounds which, like the Icelandic *álagablettur*, may not be damaged; but also of the flint arrowheads that are mentioned so often in witch trials and that the fairies use to kill cattle for food. With its wealth of detail, Kirk's *The Secret Commonwealth* is one of our most important sources for ideas about fairies in Scotland in the early modern period and contains early examples of many of the motifs that were to emerge with greater clarity only at a much later date. He reports that after the

11. The Minister's Tree at Doon Hill, Aberfoyle, Scotland, which today has become associated with the 'Fairy Minister' Robert Kirk, with messages left for the fairies.

members of a household have all gone to bed, brownies tidy up the kitchen and do the washing-up. Brownies later play a significant role in the folktales of Scotland and of wide areas of England, but it is clear from Kirk's treatise that these figures can look back on a much older history.

Kirk is important, however, not just as an early witness of British ideas about fairies, inasmuch as one of his principal aims was to describe contemporary beliefs in Scotland: he also pursued a further goal, which, in his own estimation, was arguably even more important. By describing the proven dealings with fairies on the part of his own Scottish congregation, he wanted to demonstrate that the religious scepticism of his age was misguided. For Kirk, Scotland's fairies were proof positive that atheism was a false doctrine. As a minister of the Scottish Church in the closing years of the country's witch trials, he was conscious of the risks that he was running with his benevolent view of the secret commonwealth of fairies. The *Daemonologie* of James VI had likewise taken as its starting point the reality of fairy experiences; but with all the authority of his royal prerogative, James had dismissed them as a satanic illusion. As a result, *The Secret Commonwealth* not only describes folk beliefs among the population of Gaelic Scotland: it also interweaves those beliefs with detailed arguments designed to demonstrate that a belief in fairies is not only rational and sensible, but also in keeping with the teachings of the Bible. Kirk introduced his study with no fewer than six quotations from the Bible, and later returned repeatedly to the question as to why the existence of this 'secret commonwealth' could be reconciled with both the Bible and the current state of philosophy and science. He also argued that it was not a sin for people with 'second sight' – the gift of seeing the future – to observe the fairy world around them.

Although Kirk was a member of the ruling elite, he developed an entirely new way of looking at the common people's beliefs. Far from being judgemental, he adopted an approach that sought, by means of great erudition, to legitimize popular belief and, at the same time, to use this to defend his own religious convictions. The rural minister appropriated the beliefs of the common folk and treated them as an authoritative source of the truth, in that way anticipating an approach that was not to become socially acceptable until the Age of Romanticism in the nineteenth century, when it came to appeal to a wider cross-section of the educated urban population. But Kirk was so far ahead of his time that it is no surprise to learn that, according to local legend, he never really died, instead being spirited away to fairyland in 1692, at the end of his life on earth.

Urban Elves and Fairies

CHAPTER 5

BETWEEN SCHOLARSHIP, POETRY AND PAINTING

The Urban Elves of the Nineteenth Century

The previous chapters have retraced the cultural history of elves and fairies as they left their rural lives further and further behind them. The elves and fairies of Iceland and Ireland were part of a quintessentially rural world that was home to a peasant population. The romances about King Arthur relocated the focus of their fairies' lives from rural farmsteads to the courts of knights and the aristocracy, while in the early modern period Edmund Spenser's *The Faerie Queene* and the plays of William Shakespeare led to a further shift in focus from a courtly audience to an urban one. One part of this development was Robert Kirk's *The Secret Commonwealth*, which Kirk wrote as the minister of a rural parish, but which was aimed, rather, at learned circles in London.

The following chapter introduces us to urban elves. With the Industrial Revolution, which began in Great Britain in the late eighteenth century, the urban population began to dominate social life to a hitherto unprecedented degree. The evolution of people's image of fairies was no exception here. The following pages will start by examining the rise of the modern picture of fairies as winged creatures, a development that we can first observe in London's artist circles. I shall then discuss the way in which the rise of folklore studies by urban scholars helped to make the traditional narrative repertory of the rural population accessible to the middle classes. Victorian fairy paintings will illustrate how the image of urban fairies found completely new forms of expression. The chapter will end with a section introducing developments not only in Germany in the Age of Romanticism, but also in Ireland at the time of that country's struggle to break free from the bonds of the British Empire.

Artistic Innovations in the Eighteenth Century: Fairy Wings

The elves and fairies of Old Norse literature, of Icelandic and Irish popular legend, of Arthurian literature, of the Scottish witch trials and, finally, of Shakespeare's plays all have one thing in common: they are wingless. Nowadays, by contrast, every child (and even every adult) imagines fairies as little creatures with the wings of butterflies or dragonflies. These wings are the most characteristic feature of our present-day picture of such fairies; and yet, from a historical point of view, these wings are a late accretion.

Fairy wings probably derive indirectly from Switzerland. One of the most influential natural philosophers of the early modern period was Theophrastus Bombastus von Hohenheim (1493/94–1541) from the canton of Schwyz. Better known as Paracelsus, he wrote a book in around 1530 with the title *Liber de nymphis, sylphis, pygmaeis et salamandris* (*Book of Nymphs, Sylphs, Pygmies and Salamanders*) that includes a systematic study of elemental spirits, in which he ascribed four classes of beings to the four different elements: nymphs were ascribed to water, sylphs to the air, pygmies (or gnomes) to the earth and salamanders to fire. By far the bulk of this system was Paracelsus's own invention, including the word *sylph* and the association between this creature and the element of air. Over the following centuries, his system proved immensely influential and, thanks to French esoteric writings, the idea of sylphs as elemental spirits of the air reached the English poet Alexander Pope (1688–1744) in the early eighteenth century. In a passage in *The Rape of the Lock* of 1712, Pope describes a flight of sylphs whose 'Insect-Wings' glitter in the rays of the sun with a kaleidoscopic range of different colours:

> Some to the Sun their Insect-Wings unfold,
> Waft on the Breeze, or sink in Clouds of Gold.
> Transparent Forms, too fine for mortal Sight,
> Their fluid Bodies half dissolv'd in Light
> . . .
> While ev'ry Beam new transient Colours flings,
> Colours that change whene'er they wave their Wings.[1]

It is no longer possible to say where Pope got the idea of giving wings to his sylphs, as neither Paracelsus nor the sources to which Pope may have had access mention wings in the context of these spirits of the air. Perhaps they were Pope's own creative contribution to the iconography of the period. All that we can say for certain is that as one of the most popular poets of his age, Pope popularized sylphs not only as elemental spirits of the air, but also as creatures with wings. This was to have far-reaching, long-term consequences, because by 1780 sylphs and fairies had merged in English art and literature, allowing Pope's sylphs to bequeath their wings to the fairies of a later generation.

A key role in this process was played by a group of artists that was active in London in the decades around 1800. In the eighteenth century – the Age of Enlightenment, with its emphasis on rationality and reason – depictions of elves and fairies played no more than a marginal role in the visual arts. This was an age when the prevailing aesthetic was Classicism, which took its cue from Graeco-Roman antiquity, when there was no place for fairies. By the end of the eighteenth century, however, Classicism was being supplanted by Romanticism, with its celebration of the values of natural beauty and of feelings and emotions, instead of mere rationality. No less important were artistic creativity and the tendency to venerate wildness, the mythical and sometimes even the sinister. Hand in hand with this development went a renewed interest in elves and fairies, an interest ushered in by painters such as William Blake (1757–1827), Thomas Stothard (1755–1834) and Johann Heinrich Füssli (1741–1825). Füssli was born in Switzerland, but emigrated to England at an early age and achieved fame and fortune there as Henry Fuseli. At a time when the subject elicited little interest, these three painters introduced elves and fairies into their works on a grand scale, and as pioneers in the field of fairy painting, they struck out in what, from an artistic point of view, was an entirely new direction. There was no established iconography of elves and fairies at this time, with the result that all three of these painters could decide how they wanted to depict these beings. It was only while they were elaborating this theme that they started to portray elves and fairies with wings, in the process establishing this as the most common way of depicting these beings.

The interest that this group of painters took in fairies stemmed from a deep-seated fascination with the subject. With his profound propensity for mysticism, William Blake was active not only as a painter, but also as a poet, with fairies featuring frequently in his writings. In his view of the cosmos, fairies occupied a position of enormous significance: as an admirer of Paracelsus, he repeatedly described them as elemental beings, not least in his epic poems *Milton* (1804–8) and *Jerusalem: The Emanation of the Giant Albion* (1804–20). At the same time, however, his fairies are tiny: his poem *Europe: A Prophecy* (1794) features a fairy sitting on a tulip. His fascination with fairies seems to have gone far beyond the mere desire to give them literary and artistic expression: according to one contemporary anecdote, he once said that he had seen these tiny creatures in person, and described to a female acquaintance how he had witnessed a fairy funeral one evening in his garden, when he had observed 'a procession of creatures of the size and colour of green and grey grasshoppers, bearing a body laid out on a rose-leaf, which they buried with songs, and then disappeared'.[2]

In his paintings, Blake depicted fairies in a variety of ways. A watercolour illustration for Shakespeare's *A Midsummer Night's Dream* titled *Oberon, Titania and Puck with Fairies Dancing* and dating from around 1786 depicts a whole group of fairies. Here neither Puck nor any of the fairies has wings, although one of the fairies has butterfly wings in her hair, while Puck has pointed ears – a depiction that looks forward to the idea, familiar to today's audiences, that all elves have pointed ears. On the other hand, one of the plates in Blake's *Songs of Innocence and of Experience* of 1789 presents us with the modern picture of a fairy as a winged creature: here the iconography is already fully developed (Illus. 12). The illustration shows a mother with an infant on her lap, while in front of her there is a smaller, female fairy in a yellow dress. The fairy has bright-blue butterfly wings. The entire group of figures is depicted inside a red flower.

Neither Blake nor his contemporaries developed an iconography that was valid for every fairy, and even within the same

12. A fairy depicted by William Blake in his *Songs of Innocence and of Experience* (1789).

image it was possible to depict fairies in different ways – a point well made by a famous illustration by Fuseli that portrays a scene from *A Midsummer Night's Dream* and that is now in Zürich's Kunsthaus: *Titania, Bottom and the Fairies* (1793/94). (An earlier oil painting on the same subject now hangs in Tate Britain in London.) Here the fairy queen is depicted as a human woman gently stroking her human lover, Bottom, who is the same size as she is. Above her and to one side is a wingless fairy in human form, but around a third of the size of a human. Other fairies are depicted dancing and making music in front of Titania, but these are only a few inches tall. Most of these little female figures are human in their appearance, only their size setting them apart. But there is one fairy who combines a human body with an insect's head and an insect's wings (Illus. 13). In other words, the painters who were working in London in the years around 1800 did not have any fixed ideas on what elves and fairies should look like, but introduced new possibilities into their depiction of them, adding a fresh element to the cultural history of elves and fairies and leaving a lasting mark on the subject.

The Rise of Folkloristics as a Scholarly Discipline

A further, somewhat later milestone in the cultural history of elves and fairies was the rise of folkloristics as an academic discipline in the early nineteenth century. Like fairy paintings, the study of folklore was a child of Romanticism and replaced classical Greece and Rome as models with a return to more local roots. What this meant above all was a fascination with the culture of the common folk and a new and effusive enthusiasm for the Middle Ages.

Among the most influential figures from this period were the brothers Jacob (1785–1863) and Wilhelm (1786–1859)

13. A grotesque fairy with wings and an insect's head: a detail from Henry Fuseli's painting *Titania, Bottom and the Fairies* (1793/94).

Grimm. As young students at the University of Marburg they came into contact with the Romantic poet Clemens Brentano, who inspired in them a passion for folk poetry. In the course of their long and extremely productive lives as scholars, this initial impetus was to turn the brothers into pioneers in several fields of research. Among these, arguably the best known is their work in establishing folklore as a subject for serious scientific enquiry. In this regard, their principal work

– and their lasting legacy – was their collection of fairytales (*Kinder- und Hausmärchen*), the first edition of which appeared in two volumes in 1812 and 1815. Over the course of their lifetime, they continued to expand this collection and to publish revised editions, until it finally incorporated more than two hundred tales, many of them orally transmitted. As such, this anthology was the first scholarly collection of tales from an oral tradition. When combined with the brothers' notes and ancillary studies, this edition laid the foundations for the scientific study of folklore and for research into popular storytelling as an academic discipline.

Between 1823 and 1826, the first English translation of the Grimms' fairytales appeared under the title *German Popular Tales*, thereby ensuring that the brothers' influence extended beyond the boundaries of the German-speaking world. Its publication fell on fertile ground in Britain. There Romanticism was now in full swing and had already assimilated several ideas from the German-speaking world. A good example of this development is Sir Walter Scott (1771–1832), who is widely regarded as the inventor of the historical novel and who played a key role in Britain in fuelling the Romantics' enthusiasm for the Middle Ages. He had translated Goethe's *Götz von Berlichingen* as early as 1799, and three years later enjoyed enormous success with his *Minstrelsy of the Scottish Border*, which included versions of the aforementioned ballads of Tam Lin and Thomas the Rhymer and thus ultimately helped to popularize fairy stories from the late Middle Ages.

The greatest debt that we owe the Brothers Grimm is that they prepared the way for the practice of methodical fieldwork. As the earliest representatives of the modern discipline of folkloristics, they also collected folktales that were orally transmitted. The people they approached often belonged to middle-class circles; but in at least a handful of cases they were members of the 'folk', in the sense of the less-privileged sections of society. The 'Fairy Minister' Robert Kirk had already anticipated this approach in *The Secret Commonwealth*; but whereas Kirk's activities as a collector were completely ignored by his contemporaries, the Brothers Grimm established a new paradigm that was developed and refined by their pupils. In this way they laid the foundations for the work of folklore collectors who were to become a fixed part of the cultural life of the nineteenth century.

Collections of fairytales and legends in the form of printed editions opened up the oral accounts of the 'folk' to well-to-do, urban, middle-class readers with an interest in literature. Here the international networks of the academic world played an important role. Thomas Crofton Croker (1798–1854) published the first volume of his *Fairy Legends and Traditions of the South of Ireland* as early as 1825. Generally seen as the first collection of British folktales to be based on fieldwork, it includes early examples of such popular tales as the 'Brewery of Eggshells' mentioned in Chapter 2. Among its first readers were Jacob and Wilhelm Grimm, who within a year had published a German translation under the title *Irische Elfenmärchen* (*Irish Fairytales*), which they prefaced with a treatise on fairies that ran to a hundred pages. In turn, this was taken up by Croker, who added a dedication to the Grimms to the third volume of his *Fairy Legends* when it appeared in 1828, while at the same time including an English translation of the Grimms' introduction. Croker's *Fairy Legends* thus illustrate the close international links that existed within the world of scholarship in the nineteenth century. Croker's collection was an important source of inspiration for English-language writers of the later nineteenth and early twentieth centuries. It went through numerous editions in the course of the century and had an enormous impact in Ireland and England, while at the same time illustrating the extent to which the folklore research of this period was a part of the wider world of international scholarship.

These international networks of folktale research extended to other parts of Europe. In this context, an important intermediary role was played by the German student of Scandinavian studies, Konrad Maurer (1823–1902), who for a time had studied with Jacob Grimm. Maurer visited Iceland in 1858 and, following his mentor's example, collected a number of Icelandic folktales, which he published two years later in his book *Isländische Volkssagen der Gegenwart* (*Icelandic Folktales of the Present Day*), one of the first modern studies of folk beliefs in Iceland. It includes a number of folktales about the Hidden People. Even more important was the fact that Maurer made it possible for the Icelandic scholar Jón Árnason to publish a two-volume collection of Icelandic folktales with a Leipzig firm of publishers: his *Íslenzkar þjóðsögur og æfintýri* (*Icelandic Legends and Fairytales*) appeared between 1862 and 1864 and remains one of the most comprehensive collections of traditional Icelandic folktales.

The rise of folklore as an academic discipline and the publication of fairytales and collections of folktales constituted a turning point in the cultural history of elves and fairies. Narrative material that had previously been transmitted only in oral form among the rural, peasant population now found its way into the salons and studies of the urban middle classes and became available as a major source of inspiration for writers and visual artists. In this way the traditions of the rural population that had previously been regarded with a certain degree of condescension now rose in people's estimation. But this material also underwent a profound change at the hands of the urban middle classes and was adapted to suit the new context in which it now found itself.

Between Folktale, Art and Literature: Fairy Enthusiasm in Victorian Britain

At first sight, there appears to be an unbridgeable social gulf between the world of folktales and that of art and literature. In its classic sense, the folktale belongs to what, for the most part, was the underprivileged rural population, whereas art and literature are traditionally found among members of the relatively wealthy middle classes, who regard art and literature as leisure-time activities. This is especially true of the cultural history of elves and fairies. With their fragile insect wings and insect size, the fairies that feature in the paintings of Blake and Fuseli, and that were 'modern' in their own day, were worlds apart from the elves of popular belief as researched by a new generation of folklorists, including the Brothers Grimm and Croker. This was also clear to contemporaries. In their introduction to their edition of Croker's Irish fairy stories, Jacob and Wilhelm Grimm stated categorically – and correctly – that '[n]o genuine tradition gives wings to the fairies.' Croker concurred, taking this sentence over into his English translation of the Grimms' essay.

But artists and scholars frequented the same social circles and could never be entirely divorced from one another. As a result, Croker included in his anthology an anecdote that Fuseli recalled about a fairy sighting in the middle of London, illustrating the way in which an artist's ideas passed directly into the work of a folklorist. It comes as no surprise, therefore, to discover that, despite the text's statement to the contrary, the illustrations that appeared in Croker's *Fairy Legends* included winged fairies (Illus. 14). In art and literature – and even in scholarly writings – folktale motifs were invariably adapted to suit not only the expectations of the reading public, but also the prevailing conditions in the world of urban literature. This may explain a topos that is already found in Kipling's *Puck of Pook's Hill* (1906) and in many of today's works of fantasy fiction, according to which elves do not like to be described as fairies and hate being compared to the winged creatures found in so many children's books.

In this way Romanticism created a situation in which a whole new range of motifs and stories was opened up to literature and art, while at the same time contemporaries had no hesitation in reworking these motifs to suit their needs and

14. An illustration from the third volume of Thomas Crofton Croker's *Fairy Legends and Traditions of the South of Ireland* (1828), showing two fairies with dragonfly or butterfly wings dancing on a flower.

interests, some of these reworkings proving to be particularly free. In the Great Britain over which Queen Victoria reigned from 1837 until 1901, this led to an extraordinary popularity of the fairy motif. It was during these decades that the Industrial Revolution began to affect people's lives in far-reaching ways. An iconic symbol of this transformation was the opening up of the railway network that began in the 1830s and that soon became one of the most important signs of technological progress. In the natural sciences, Charles Darwin developed the modern theory of evolution in his book *On the Origin of Species* (1859), in the process calling into question the Bible's teachings on creation. These deep-seated changes in technology and culture altered people's lives at an altogether unprecedented speed, giving rise in Victorian Britain to a widespread feeling that this was indeed an age of progress and of modernity.

But it was unclear where this progress might lead, resulting, in turn, in worries and fears – not least because it was soon hard to ignore the widespread environmental damage caused by heavy industry and the wretched conditions in which the new working class was obliged to live. Hand in hand with thoughts on progress went a nostalgic longing for a transfigured past: the railways may have symbolized progress, but time and again it was claimed that the noise of the locomotives had driven the fairies from the English countryside. This tension between a belief in progress and a worried sense of nostalgia pervaded the whole of Victorian life and found expression in the omnipresence of elves and fairies in the arts and crafts, and in painting, theatre and literature.

A Victorian genre that was especially characteristic of this development was fairy painting. Between the 1830s and the 1870s, countless paintings, drawings, prints and book illustrations were produced in Great Britain, taking elves and fairies as their theme. These images of fairies perpetuated the iconographical conventions of Blake and Fuseli, but whereas Blake and Fuseli had been pioneers who, for the most part, stood alone in the arts scene of their time, images of elves and fairies now became a subject for mass culture. For several decades they were so popular that everyone who picked up a paint brush and envisaged a career as a painter would find themselves painting fairies. Indeed, some artists devoted themselves solely to this subject at this time.

One of the British artists who became known above all for his fairy paintings was John Anster Fitzgerald (1819/23–1906) who, starting in 1845, exhibited his works on a regular basis at the Royal Academy in London. Time and again, his paintings depict people asleep and dreaming of elves and fairies. In these paintings the sleepers are repeatedly surrounded by entire hordes of fairies, some of them as translucent as glass, while others are depicted with a keen eye for physical detail. On rare occasions, a fairy is portrayed as a beautiful figure in human form, but with a butterfly's wings. Most, however, are depicted as grotesquely deformed beings, whose faces and limbs often bear insect-like features. Fitzgerald also repeatedly introduced references to drug use into his paintings. In *The Artist's Dream* (1857), a painter dreams of capturing a beautiful fairy on his canvas, while an animal-like translucent being offers the sleeping artist a glass filled with a liquid of a dubious nature. A watercolour titled *The Nightmare* (*c.* 1857/58) depicts a sleeping woman, on whose bedside table two empty phials can be seen. Around her are visions of a lovesick tragedy and grotesque translucent figures, with some animal-featured beings carrying trays of drinking glasses and a steaming bowl. In pictures like these, fairies are beings from a world between sleep and waking, a world of nightmares that can be entered through the consumption of hallucinogenic substances.

Even when Fitzgerald does not explicitly depict a nightmare, his portrayal of fairies remains ambivalent, a point well illustrated by an undated watercolour titled *Fairy Hordes Attacking a Bat* (Illus. 15). At the centre of the image, the observer can see a bat lit from behind by a full moon and with dense foliage beneath it. The bat is directly in front of the moon, its wings fully open, its extended ears suggesting a sense of mild surprise. It can be seen flying towards the dense leaves of a bush, where at least a dozen fairies lie in wait. All of the fairies have insect wings, and around half have human bodies and appear to be wearing armour made from petals and parts of plants. The others have insect-like limbs and corresponding heads. Both the human fairies and the others that tend, rather, to resemble insects are carrying thorns designed to serve as spears. Even more of them can be seen in vague outline in the distance and likewise appear to be on the point of joining the hunt. For the bat there is no escape.

The fairies in this watercolour that are shaped like humans are depicted as beautiful, dainty figures that could be any

15. John Anster Fitzgerald's *Fairy Hordes Attacking a Bat* (undated).

gender. The floral elements in their clothing give them an air of delicate charm. These lovely creatures raise their spears of thorn with the aim of attacking the bat, and yet their facial expressions retain their cheerful composure. They are beautiful, happy, lethal hunters without a vestige of pity for their victim, which they will skewer in a spirit of light-hearted, blissful serenity. Fitzgerald's fairies may be small and they may wear petals on their heads, but nice they are not. They embody an unequal confluence of beauty, nature, cruelty and ugliness which, in spite of the elements of loveliness that it reveals, never runs the risk of descending into saccharine kitsch.

An alternative kind of ambiguity is achieved by strikingly different means in the fairy paintings of Richard Doyle (1824–83), whose family had close links with the cultural history of elves and fairies. His younger brother, Charles Altamont Doyle (1832–93), also painted fairies, recording the nightmarish visions that led to his being held in a secure psychiatric unit towards the end of his life. Charles was also the father of Sir Arthur Conan Doyle, to whom we shall return in due course. Richard made a name for himself not least as an illustrator working for books and magazines. It was in this context that he produced his best-known work, a volume of plates with the title *In Fairy Land: A Series of Pictures from the Elf-World*. First published in 1870, this volume combines Doyle's illustrations with a poem by William Allingham that reproduces the conversations said to be held by fairies over the course of a day, but only loosely related to the images. Doyle's colour plates represented a high point of the art of printing at that time. The fairies who are depicted in this series of images are creatures with human bodies, but with the proportions of children. Some of them have the wings of a butterfly.

At first sight, Doyle's depiction of fairies as small – or even tiny – children makes them seem harmless and cute, in which regard they reflect the rise of children's books in the 1860s and later, many of which are all about elves and fairies. The plate 'Triumphal March of the Elf-King', for example, leaves the impression of a high-spirited procession, in which a relatively ill-disciplined retinue of elves and fairies can be seen skipping, flying, riding and marching behind the Elf-King, while the Elf-King himself is a comic character whose hair and beard are so long that four pageboys are needed to carry them (Illus. 16). But a closer inspection requires this initial, light-hearted impression to be modified: throughout this image of boisterously carefree goings-on, Doyle has included elves that can be seen mistreating the animals on which they are riding. One elf strikes his whip against the horns of a snail that is being ridden by another elf. A second can be observed pulling a muskrat by its tail, while a third administers a vicious kick to a tiny beetle. A fourth elf appears to use his fist to strike the bird on which he is sitting. In this way the

16. Richard Doyle's 'Triumphal March of the Elf-King' (1870).

apparently childlike innocence of the elfin world is disturbed by the sort of casual cruelty that is also found in some of the other illustrations that appear in the pages of *In Fairy Land*.

One of the more tragic figures of Victorian fairy painting was Richard Dadd (1817–86). His talent was discovered at an early age, and he was still only in his mid-twenties when he found in Sir Thomas Phillips a patron who made it possible for him to travel to the Middle East. But the physical and mental strain of this journey had a huge impact on Dadd's state of mind, and in August 1843 he suffered a nervous breakdown, during which he became so convinced that his father was the Devil that he murdered him. Following his arrest, he was diagnosed as schizophrenic and spent the rest of his life in a series of psychiatric institutions.

Between 1855 and 1864, while he was being detained at the Bethlem Royal Hospital – popularly known as Bedlam – he created his masterpiece, *The Fairy Feller's Master-Stroke* (Illus. 17). Transferred to another asylum – at Broadmoor – he wrote a poem to go with the painting, which shows a group of fairies in a forest of grass and daisies. Each of the fairies is the size of a daisy. All have human form, but their proportions are often distorted. In the top third of the painting, Oberon and Titania can be seen holding court. Both are wearing crowns and Titania has the wings of a butterfly. In the centre of the lower two thirds of the painting is the 'fairy feller', his axe poised to strike a hazelnut. With raised hand, a bearded magician in the very centre of the image gives him a sign to attempt his 'masterstroke' and split the nut with a single blow of his axe.

As a result of Dadd's lifelong incarceration in psychiatric asylums, this extremely detailed and surreal image remained unknown and was not publicly exhibited until 1935. Since

17. A detail from Richard Dadd's *The Fairy Feller's Master-Stroke* (1855–64).

then, however, it has become arguably the most famous of all Victorian fairy paintings, and regularly features in literary works today. In 2011, Alex Bledsoe published the first volume (*The Hum and the Shiver*) in what is currently a six-volume series of novels known generically as the *Tufa Novels*; the series takes Dadd's painting as its starting point. Eight years earlier, Terry Pratchett had written a literary adaptation of it in *The Wee Free Men*. Victorian fairy painters created an artificial elfin world in which the creatures that had previously had their roots in popular rural beliefs were wrenched from that context and sent off in an entirely new direction that was to have an extraordinarily far-reaching impact. An element of the grotesque now came to the fore – an element that may have existed in inchoate form in older popular traditions, but which had never been as dominant as it was now.

At the same time, mortals and fairies grew ever more distant. For Robert Kirk, fairies had been the 'good neighboures' of humans, but thanks to Doyle's *In Fairy Land*, they were now spirited away to a world – 'Fairy Land' – that was divorced from its human counterpart. Although the word 'fairyland' had already appeared in Shakespeare's *A Midsummer Night's Dream*, it was only now that in their dreams humans imagined fairies living in a completely different world. In this way, the fairies of Victorian Britain laid the foundations for our present-day view of elves and fairies.

Other Countries, Other Fairies: Germany and Ireland

While elves and fairies were evolving into one of the most striking of all artistic themes in Victorian Britain, their reception in the German-speaking world remained relatively muted. Arguably, this was due to the fact that in Britain elves and fairies were regarded as an autochthonous, profoundly British object of interest, while most of the reactions to fairies in the German-speaking world rested on the more or less successful adaptation of international motifs designed to meet the expectations of German-speaking audiences.

This dependence of German elves and fairies on international influences even extended as far as the terms themselves: as noted earlier, the German word *Fee* was an eighteenth-century borrowing from the French *fée*, while the German term *Elf* derives from the English *elf*. The word *Elf* was first used in 1742 by the Swiss writer and translator Johann Jakob Bodmer (1698–1783) in his translation of Milton's *Paradise Lost*, before becoming established thanks to the 1764 translation of

Shakespeare's *A Midsummer Night's Dream* by Christoph Martin Wieland (1733–1813). German already had its own word, *Alb* or *Alp*, which is cognate with English *elf* and Old Norse *álfr*, but by the eighteenth century this term had receded so far into the distance that it was almost entirely replaced by the loan-words *Elf* and *Fee*, surviving only in a handful of compounds, such as *Alptraum*, literally an 'elf dream', or nightmare. In short, the elves and fairies that are found in art and literature in the German-speaking world can be described as autochthonous to only a limited extent. They were taken over as international motifs, but were rarely treated in the sort of way that might have influenced international currents in cultural history.

A particularly striking example of the way in which German texts about elves were dependent on foreign-language influences is Goethe's ballad *Erlkönig*. The motif of the Erl-King entered German literature with a ballad that Johann Gottfried Herder (1744–1803) published in 1779 under the title *Erlkönigs Tochter* (*Erl-King's Daughter*), which tells of how an elfin woman who is the daughter of the Erl-King tries to lure the knight Sir Oluf into her bed, and of how she brings about his death when he refuses. Herder's poem was a reworking of a Danish ballad, *Her Oluf hand rider saa vide*, which for its part was known by the seventeenth century at the latest, but which can ultimately be traced back to the tradition of the Old French *lais*. In his own reworking of the text, Herder did not translate the phrase 'Eller-Kongens daatter' literally as 'Tochter des Elfenkönigs' ('daughter of the elf king') but as 'Erlkönigs Tochter' ('Erl-King's daughter'), thus turning the Danish fairy king into a new figure – the Erl-King, who gave his name to Herder's ballad.

Only a few years later, this new figure of the Erl-King inspired Johann Wolfgang von Goethe (1749–1832) to write his own ballad *Erlkönig* in 1782. Goethe's poem describes a father's attempt to save his young son from the Erl-King, who tries to lure the child to a realm where games, dances, brightly coloured flowers and the Erl-King's daughters await the boy. Although the Erl-King is unable to take the lad, he dies in his father's arms. As such, the ballad is a free reworking of the familiar motif of the abduction of children by fairies. But the use of a new word, 'Erl-King', severed the link with elves and fairies. Goethe's *Erlkönig* soon established itself as one of the most successful of all German ballads and continued to leave its mark on other art forms: quite apart from a large number of paintings and book illustrations, there is also a statue in Jena and more than a dozen musical settings, most famously one composed in 1815 by Franz Schubert (1797–1828). But by removing the elves from this elfin tale, *Erlkönig* is also something of a dead-end in terms of the reception history of fairies.

Another example illustrates how German literature of the nineteenth century was able to assimilate ideas from abroad, while failing to take that material – in this case of English provenance – and point it in a fundamentally new direction. In 1834, Ludwig Uhland (1787–1862) published a ballad under the title *Das Glück von Edenhall* (*The Luck of Edenhall*), which describes the downfall of the lords of Edenhall. They had once received a crystal beaker as a gift from a fairy (Uhland uses the word *Fei*), but it came with the threat that Edenhall's good fortune would end if the glass were ever to break. An ebullient young laird tempts fate by using the chalice at a drinking session and chinking glasses with it in a particularly violent way. The glass breaks and that same night the laird's enemies burn down his castle.

Uhland's ballad is a reworking of a motif familiar from the second volume of Scott's *Minstrelsy of the Scottish Border* of 1802. Here Scott had reported on a tradition in the Musgrave family, whose home was at Edenhall in Cumberland. One of their forebears – or, according to another version of the tale, one of their servants – had once stumbled upon a fairy banquet and stolen one of the fairies' goblets, on which the fairies had then laid a curse:

If this cup either break or fall
Farewell the Luck of Edenhall![3]

Known as the 'Luck of Edenhall', this goblet still exists in the form of a magnificent beaker decorated in coloured enamel and probably made in Syria or Egypt in the fourteenth century (Illus. 18). It was donated to London's Victoria and Albert Museum in 1926. Eight years later, the old family seat of Eden Hall was torn down.

Uhland's poem familiarized German-speaking audiences with this exceptional object, and even enjoyed a certain international impact thanks to an English translation made by the American poet Henry Wadsworth Longfellow (1807–82). But it contributed nothing substantially new to the evolving image of elves and fairies, tending rather to exemplify the fact that German-language responses to fairies were largely limited to the adaptation of foreign-language originals. Even so, the German-speaking world was closely integrated into the world of international art and culture. One example of this is a deluxe two-volume edition of *The Book of British Ballads* by S.C. Hall (the pen-name of the Irish writer Anna Maria Hall (1800–81)) that was published in 1844 and that included an English ballad titled *The Luck of Edenhall*. This edition was dedicated to Ludwig I of Bavaria. In other words, the German-speaking world remained a part of the European cultural history of elves and fairies, and fairies provided the subject matter for a whole series of well-known writers and composers, from Ludwig Tieck's literary fairytale *Die Elfen*

18. The 'Luck of Edenhall', glass beaker decorated in enamel (fourteenth century).

(*The Elves*) of 1797 and Heinrich Heine's 1827 poem 'Dämmernd liegt der Sommerabend' ('Glimm'ring lies the summer even') about a beautiful fairy bathing in a moonlit stream, to Wagner's early opera *Die Feen* (*The Fairies*), which was completed in 1834 but not performed until 1888, five years after his death. But after the pioneering work that Jacob and Wilhelm Grimm had done in laying the foundations for folkloristic research into the world of elves and fairies, the German-speaking world produced few other ideas that were to have any more far-reaching impact.

In Ireland, conversely, the cultural history of elves and fairies evolved along very different lines. Here the research into folktales pioneered by the Brothers Grimm was to have important repercussions. Folklore research and literature were both to enjoy a golden age within the context of Irish attempts to gain independence from British rule. Two key figures in this development were Lady Gregory (1852–1932) and William Butler Yeats (1865–1939), both of whom wrote works of lasting importance on Irish fairy stories and made outstanding contributions to Irish literature in general.

Augusta, Lady Gregory was born in 1852 as Isabella Augusta Persse, but for the most part she published under the name of Lady Gregory. Her family owned lands in County Galway and belonged to Ireland's social elite. Despite her family's close links with England, she sided with the Irish in their attempts to assert their own cultural identity and gain political independence from British rule. She was a central figure in the establishment of the Irish Literary Theatre in 1899 and the Abbey Theatre in 1904, in that way playing a major role in the literary revival of the late nineteenth and early twentieth centuries, whose pioneers pursued the goal of creating a cultural identity of their own.

Fairies were important to Lady Gregory both through her interest in medieval Irish literature and as beings that were a part of the popular beliefs of her own day. Her book *Gods and Fighting Men* (1904) is of significance not least for its free translations of medieval Irish texts in which the Túatha Dé Danann play a central role (see Chapter 2). In this way, tales about the medieval forebears of fairies became accessible for the first time to a wider public, in a readily available format. In mediating medieval traditions in this way, Lady Gregory had a profound influence on the imagery of the Celtic Revival. Outside any purely literary context, perhaps the most famous sign of the cultural impact of this contribution on Lady Gregory's part was the 1911 painting *The Riders of the Sidhe* by John Duncan (1866–1945). Here we see a group of fairies from the Túatha Dé Danann riding out on magnificently caparisoned horses, Duncan's style recalling the images of medieval knights in Arthurian literature (Illus. 19).

In addition to her work in making medieval Irish tales available to a wider audience, Lady Gregory also established a reputation for herself as an important collector of traditional narratives, more especially from the Gaelic-speaking West of Ireland. Her abiding legacy in this field is her two-volume *Visions and Beliefs in the West of Ireland* (1920), an edition that marks the culmination of her activities as a collector of Irish folk traditions. This was a collection that she had begun to assemble in the 1890s through her work with the poorer sections of society. The fairies or Good People play a central role in many of these traditions, and in her books Lady Gregory repeatedly emphasized that for the Gaelic-speaking rural population these beings represented a very real facet of their everyday lives. Many people still claimed to see them and to have experienced their powers at first hand.

Lady Gregory also influenced the work of William Butler Yeats, who, widely regarded as one of the greatest

19. John Duncan's *The Riders of the Sidhe* (1911).

English-speaking poets of the twentieth century, received the Nobel Prize for Literature in 1923. They shared a passion for the world of Irish folktales and, like Lady Gregory, Yeats published anthologies of Irish tales: *Fairy and Folk Tales of the Irish Peasantry* appeared in 1888 and *Irish Fairy Tales* in 1892. The two first met in 1898, a meeting that turned into a lifelong friendship, one of the consequences of which was that the aristocratic Lady Gregory became Yeats's patron, supporting him financially.

Above and beyond his familiarity with traditional Irish storytelling, Yeats also developed his own transfiguring view of the fairy world. One of his most famous poems is 'The Stolen Child' (1889), which takes as its starting point the motif of a child's abduction by fairies. The theft of children and their replacement by changelings was one of the main themes of contemporary popular legend and is found again and again in Lady Gregory's collection; but whereas popular legend focuses on the horrors of an event that destroys families and drives parents to the brink of despair, Yeats's poem is primarily concerned with the temptations of the fairy world and with the lure of an idyll of nature in which the child can escape from the world's miseries. The opening stanza reads:

> Where dips the rocky highland
> Of Sleuth Wood in the lake,
> There lies a leafy island
> Where flapping herons wake
> The drowsy water rats;
> There we've hid our faery vats,
> Full of berries,
> And of reddest stolen cherries.
> *Come away, O human child!*
> *To the waters and the wild*

> *With a faery, hand in hand,*
> *For the world's more full of weeping than you can understand.*[4]

In this poetic vision, Yeats holds out the promise of a Romantic escape from the world, even though an undertow of cruelty remains – in the following stanzas one of the fairies' games consists in giving nightmares to the trout as they sleep in the stream. But the poem's basic mood has shifted from the unspeakable suffering at the heart of the folktale to the temptation posed by an otherworld that is ambivalent and close to nature, but ultimately all too seductive.

Yeats's reason for adopting this alternative approach must be sought in his powerful predisposition towards mysticism and the occult. For Yeats, fairies in all their guises were an object of spiritual longing – a view reflected not only in his literary works, but also in his activities in the field of alternative religion. In the inaugural issue of *The Irish Theosophist* in 1892, for example, he published an article on a vision of Irish fairies that had been vouchsafed to him and his spiritual companion, named only as D.D. Here his description of fairies is entirely in the spirit of Victorian fairy painting, imagining them as grotesque creatures ascribed to the four elements of water, air, earth and fire. Yeats and D.D. regarded the fairies of earth as entities whose bodies were like the stems of flowers and whose clothes were like petals. They fed off the honey that dripped from a bush.[5] Yeats's article illustrates his attempt to subsume Irish mythology within the theosophist movement, which then had great international influence.

Between 1896 and 1902, Yeats even tried to found his own occult order, the Order of Celtic Mysteries, which was intended to be a specifically Irish variant of the occultism of his time: central to this movement were to be the Túatha Dé

Danann of the Irish tradition. In Yeats's eyes, the fairies of Irish folktales were one and the same as the Túatha Dé Danann of medieval Irish literature, because both, he believed, embodied the ancient gods of pre-Christian Ireland. In Yeats's view of the world, these creatures were one thing above all else: they were real. In a preface that he wrote for Lady Gregory's *Gods and Fighting Men*, he stressed that the reality of these divinely otherworldly beings was 'confirmed by apparitions among the country-people to-day'.[6] For Yeats, popular belief was a guarantee of spiritual truth; and since the people who held these beliefs were convinced that fairies were real, so they must indeed be real.

Yeats may have regarded folk beliefs as an absolute, but this did not prevent him from adapting their motifs to conform to his own occult vision of a national Irish identity. And although he raised popular Gaelic beliefs to the point where they came to embody an Irish national spirituality in his eyes, he had no qualms about rewriting them in the spirit of his own social and cultural surroundings. Only to the Gaelic fishermen and farmers to whom he appealed may his vision of the blandishments of the fairy world have seemed even more bewildering than the logic of British colonial rule.

CHAPTER 6

A CHANGE OF DIRECTION AFTER THE TURN OF THE CENTURY

Elves and Fairies in the Early Twentieth Century, from Peter Pan to the Fairy Investigation Society

The intermingling of folklore research on the subject of fairies and of literature and the occult in the work of Lady Gregory and W.B. Yeats that I discussed at the end of the previous chapter has brought us to the early decades of the twentieth century. Between them, Lady Gregory and Yeats exerted an enormous influence on the Irish literary scene of this period, but it was also a time that witnessed a change of direction in Great Britain – a change that was to prove significant for the cultural history of elves and fairies far beyond Britain and Ireland, continuing to resonate internationally right down to the present day. These innovations crystallized more especially in the work of J.M. Barrie and his creation of the figure of Peter Pan, but also in the affair that became known as the 'Cottingley Fairies'. This chapter will examine the role of Peter Pan and the Cottingley photographs in the cultural history of elves and fairies, both of which were to be decisive in turning the fairy realm into a world of infantile tweeness. I shall then turn my attention to the Fairy Investigation Society as a fascinating curiosity that illustrates the interdependence of literature and the history of religion, while at the same time leaving evidence of contemporary developments that remains of lasting value.

The (Almost) Definitive Infantilization of Fairies: Peter Pan and Tinker Bell

Arguably the most successful play in the whole history of children's theatre was seen for the first time at the Duke of York's Theatre in London on 27 December 1904. Its title was *Peter Pan, or The Boy Who Would Not Grow Up* (Illus. 20 and 21). The play's author was the dramatist and novelist James Matthew Barrie (1860–1937), a Scot who spent most of the second half of his life writing for the stage, in which capacity he was regarded as one of the leading playwrights of his day. His best-known work, *Peter Pan*, has an unusually complex publication history. The character appeared for the first time

20. Charles Buchel's poster advertising the original production of J.M. Barrie's children's play, *Peter Pan* (1904).

in 1902, in Barrie's novel *The Little White Bird*, which was intended for grown-ups. As a play, *Peter Pan* proved a dazzling success, the original production chalking up a run of 145 performances. Then, in 1906, Barrie took the Peter Pan chapters from *The Little White Bird* and, after subjecting them to a handful of minor revisions, published them as *Peter Pan in Kensington Gardens*, this time aimed at an audience of children. A novel with the title *Peter Pan and Wendy* appeared in 1911 and was based on the stage play, the text of which was not published until 1928. This had been preceded by the first cinema version – a silent film titled *Peter Pan*, directed by Herbert Brenon, with Betty Bronson as Peter Pan. In 1953, Walt Disney made a full-length cartoon film of *Peter Pan*, and since then a never-ending series of film adaptations and children's books has ensured that the story is now universally known. Some critics have even gone so far as to describe Barrie's *Peter Pan* as a modern myth.

The basic plot of *Peter Pan* can be summarized relatively briefly. Wendy Darling and her two brothers are visited one night in their nursery by Peter Pan, who has lost his shadow there while trying to eavesdrop on a nursery story. Wendy sews his shadow back on and, with the help of fairy dust from the fairy Tinker Bell, Peter gives the children the ability to fly and takes them with him to Never Land, where they have a series of adventures with mermaids, Native Americans and pirates, though Tinker Bell's jealousy causes problems. Ultimately, they triumph over the wicked Captain Hook and finally return to their parents' home, where their mother and father have long been desperately waiting for them.

On one level of the narrative, fairies are vital to the action, thanks not least to the figure of Tinker Bell, who plays a key role throughout the work. The huge success of Disney's

21. Pauline Chase as Peter Pan, Hilda Trevelyan as Wendy, Robb Harwood as Captain Hook and others in the production of Barrie's *Peter Pan* at the Duke of York's Theatre (December 1907).

1953 cartoon film meant that the portrayal of Tinker Bell as a tiny blonde with extremely skimpy clothing and insect-like wings is now one of the most familiar of all images of fairies. Even in this film version, which otherwise largely avoids the darker aspects of Barrie's original story, Tinker Bell retains something of the ambivalence of older ideas about fairies, according to which these creatures were neither small nor dainty, but often inscrutable and dangerous. After all, Tinker Bell is jealous of Wendy and keeps trying to get rid of her – even attempting to engineer her death in order to have Peter Pan for herself.

But myths about elves and fairies permeate Barrie's original and extend far beyond the figure of Tinker Bell. Peter Pan is the boy who will not grow up – a permanent child who lives in Never Land with the lost boys, who are described as follows in Barrie's play:

WENDY. Where do you live now?

PETER. With the lost boys.

WENDY. Who are they?

PETER. They are the children who fall out of their prams when the nurse is looking the other way. If they are not claimed in seven days they are sent far away to the Never Land. I'm captain.

WENDY. What fun it must be.

PETER (*craftily*). Yes, but we are rather lonely. You see, Wendy, we have no female companionship.

WENDY. Are none of the other children girls?

PETER. Oh no; girls, you know, are much too clever to fall out of their prams.[1]

The play does not examine the question of how it is possible simply to lose a child and not notice. As a result, the lost boys who have fallen out of their prams appear to be just one of the humorous details that are found in a text imbued with a sense of irony. The effect is enhanced by the final point that this is an example of male stupidity, when compared with female circumspection. There are repeated sideswipes of this kind in Barrie's works, since he uses humour systematically to criticize his contemporaries' views about women.

Barrie's earlier version of the story in *Peter Pan in Kensington Gardens* throws a completely different light on this passage. Here Barrie treats the character in a way that suggests both an alternative reading and a prehistory of the play. Here Peter is a child who flew out of his nursery when he was only seven days old when he heard his parents talking about his future and about his life as a grown-up. But Peter never wants to grow up, and so he flies off to Kensington Gardens, one of London's Royal Parks, where he lives with the fairies and birds. Fairies live throughout the park: as soon as its gates are closed in the evening, they emerge from their hiding places and hold magnificent balls presided over by Queen Mab. If a child falls from its pram unnoticed and remains in the park after the gates have been closed, it may lose its life to the cold or to the malice of wicked fairies, so Peter does his best to rescue these children. But sometimes he arrives too late, and then all that he can do is dig a grave for the lost boy and place a little tombstone over it.

A comparison between this particular version of the story and the stage adaptation makes it plain that falling out of one's pram is a euphemism for the death of a child, and that the 'lost boys' are dead children. It is never entirely clear what Peter himself may be, although the stories all stress that he is not entirely human. That he flies away from his nursery may imply that he, too, is one of the lost boys. This is also suggested in the stage play and, more especially, in the stage directions. When he tells Wendy that he has no mother, she attempts to take him in her arms and comfort him:

WENDY. Peter!
(*She leaps out of bed to put her arms round him, but he draws back; he does not know why, but he knows he must draw back.*)

PETER. You mustn't touch me.

WENDY. Why?

PETER. No one must ever touch me.

WENDY. Why?

PETER. I don't know.
(*He is never touched by any one in the play.*)[2]

No one is allowed to touch Peter and no one does so. A stage direction in Act Three also states that it is one of Peter's more remarkable qualities that he is weightless, but he is prevented from speaking about this. He evidently left his physical presence behind when he flew away out of his nursery.

Barrie's different versions of the subject never fully explain exactly how he flew away. In *Peter Pan in Kensington Gardens* he flies off into the park, whereas in the stage play he flies to Never Land. At first sight, Kensington Gardens and Never Land are two very different places – one of them a park in London, the other an imaginary island – but they have one thing in common: fairies live there. Tinker Bell and many other fairies whose existence is merely hinted at in the play live in Never Land, while Queen Mab holds court in Kensington Gardens. Both places are home to the incorporeal Peter Pan, who has been spirited away to the fairy world. If the sombre echoes of the phrase 'lost boys' recall dead children, then Peter's incorporeality may be explained by the fact that as a Scot, Barrie was reworking an element of the Scottish fairy tradition: as long ago as 1692, the 'Fairy Minister' Robert Kirk had noted in *The Secret Commonwealth* that many of his contemporaries believed that the souls of the dead passed into fairy mounds. None of this is explicitly stated by Barrie, but his dead children and fairies may have a common denominator in the fact that the world of the dead and the otherworld are one and the same in historical accounts from Scotland.

Barrie's work contained enough allusions to these more sombre aspects of traditional ideas about fairies in Scotland to make it likely that he was familiar with the corresponding traditions. Hidden behind the façade of this entertaining children's nursery tale we can identify a poetic contemplation of loss, grief and death, and of some of the darker aspects of the popular beliefs of the past. But Barrie has removed the sting from his material by the way in which he has reworked it, systematically trivializing the fairy world, turning it into something more twee and harmless, and driving it from the present. When Peter first tells Wendy that he knows fairies, she is profoundly impressed:

> WENDY (*with great eyes*). You know fairies, Peter!
>
> PETER (*surprised that this should be a recommendation*). Yes, but they are nearly all dead now. (*Baldly*) You see, Wendy, when the first baby laughed for the first time, the laugh broke into a thousand pieces and they all went skipping about, and that was the beginning of fairies. And now when every new baby is born its first laugh becomes a fairy. So there ought to be one fairy for every boy or girl.
>
> WENDY (*breathlessly*). Ought to be? Isn't there?
>
> PETER. Oh no. Children know such a lot now. Soon they don't believe in fairies, and every time a child says 'I don't believe in fairies' there is a fairy somewhere that falls down dead.[3]

This passage makes an explicit connection between the lives of fairies and those of babies and small children: fairies owe their existence to the laughter of infants and die as soon as these infants no longer believe in them. Here fairies are reduced from mysterious forces to an element in the world of small children. This link between childhood and the fairy world also operates in the other direction: in a coda to the stage play, Barrie suggests that when children grow up they lose their ability to see beings from the otherworld. A year after he has defeated Captain Hook, Peter visits Wendy again and is disturbed to find that she has grown much bigger, while she herself can no longer see him as clearly as she once could. Growing up closes the doors to the fairy world of Never Land.

More especially in *Peter Pan in Kensington Gardens*, Barrie's fairies are subjected to a reductive process not only by being associated with infanthood, but by being described as 'flower fairies', tiny creatures linked with flowers and flowering plants on several different levels. One fairy that plays a prominent role in the story is the Duke of Christmas Daisies, named after the flowering shrub. Queen Mab's Lord Chamberlain blows on a dandelion clock when she wants to know the time. The fairies can speed up the growth of flowers and are practically invisible to the naked eye of grown-ups because they disguise themselves as flowers as soon as they sense danger. This happened once to a group of twenty-four children from a girl's school for fairies and also to their governess when they were caught unawares by some humans. They simply stood stock-still and pretended to be hyacinths. Unfortunately, it turned out that the humans were two gardeners who were about to plant some bulbs in the bed where the hyacinth fairies were standing, so the gardeners dug up the hyacinths and took them to a garden shed, from which they escaped, unharmed, the following night, suffering only from shock and the loss of their shoes.

But even in turning his fairies into flower fairies, Barrie retains an echo of older, darker conceptions of fairies. The fairies in *Peter Pan in Kensington Gardens* love dances, and fairy rings are the visible traces of their balls that are left in the grass the next morning. Peter Pan provides the fairies with an orchestra, sitting in the middle of the fairy ring and accompanying their dancing on his flute. On one occasion he plays so magnificently that the fairy queen says she will grant him a wish. But when Peter says that he wants to see his mother, this places the fairies in a predicament: because they want to keep Peter and his music for themselves, they do everything in their power to prevent him from returning to the world of humans. And in this they succeed, even if their success rests more on Peter's mistakes than on anything that the fairies may have done. Nowhere else is the story of Peter Pan as an eternal child so clearly a variant of the themes that are found in the folktales in which fairies abduct children and carry them off to the otherworld, rarely allowing them to return home to the world of humans. The modern myth of Peter Pan is an echo of the legend of the changeling.

It is one of the ironies of the cultural history of elves and fairies that Barrie's dark and multilayered treatment of the changeling motif contributed above all to the process by which fairies were trivialized. Barrie's original texts are rarely read today, but continue to resonate, primarily through the countless adaptations in the form of children's books and films. These newer adaptations tend to stress the humorous side of a story that is made to seem all about children, whereas its deeper, more unfathomable aspects are largely overlooked. Barrie's Tinker Bell was part of a narrative tradition designed to explain inconceivable suffering; but despite all his efforts to the contrary, the Tinker Bell of the present day has become a trivial icon of the world of children's entertainment. Between 2005 and 2012, Hollywood even marketed the figure as part of its Disney Fairies franchise, giving the character her own series of films, video games, children's books and even a magazine. Despite her undying popularity, little is left of Barrie's profoundly ambivalent character.

The Cottingley Photographs

In December 1920, the Christmas edition of *The Strand* magazine ran an unexpected story headlined:

Fairies Photographed: An Epoch-Making Event Described by A. Conan Doyle

Sir Arthur Conan Doyle was the celebrated creator of the detective Sherlock Holmes and, as such, a symbol of rational

A CHANGE OF DIRECTION

thinking; but here he was found presenting photographic evidence of the actual existence of fairies. What had happened?

The events that led to this sensationalist headline had taken place only a few years earlier in the village of Cottingley, now part of the City of Bradford, in the North of England. The First World War had forced Annie Griffiths and her daughter Frances, who had grown up in South Africa, to move to England, where they lived with Annie's sister, Polly Wright. Frances shared a room in the Wrights' home with her cousin Elsie, and the two girls soon became good friends. They spent many of the hot summer days of 1917 by a beck at the bottom of their garden, and, much to her mother's annoyance, Frances regularly returned home wet and covered in mud. In answer to her furious questioning as to why the two girls had to go so often to this particular beck, Frances suddenly blurted out one day: 'To see the fairies!' Elsie agreed and insisted that she, too, had seen fairies by the stream. Their parents naturally refused to believe a word that either of the two girls said – they were then only ten and sixteen years old.

Decades later, Elsie told a reporter that she had merely wanted to comfort the angry Frances when she had the idea of borrowing her father's camera and a photographic plate and of announcing that she wanted to use them to prove that they had actually seen some fairies by the beck. Armed with the camera, Elsie and Frances had run off to the stream and within an hour returned. Elsie's father developed the photograph that very same evening: it showed Frances resting on her elbows in front of a waterfall, with a group of winged fairies dancing directly in front of her (Illus. 22).

At no point did Elsie's father, Arthur Wright, believe that this was a photograph of supernatural creatures, immediately suspecting that cardboard cut-outs had been used. Elsie and Frances, however, stuck to their story and insisted that

22. The first of the Cottingley fairy photographs: 'Frances and the Fairies' (July 1917).

they had photographed actual fairies. In September 1917 they borrowed the camera again, and this time they returned with an image of Elsie sitting on the grass while a 'gnome' danced in front of her. This might have been the end of the story, as the two girls took no further photographs, and the two that they *had* taken were treated as curios, little fuss being made of them.

But the mothers of Elsie and Frances developed an interest in theosophy, which at that time was the most important international alternative religious movement, with lodges in many British towns and cities and a programme of lectures given by peripatetic speakers that ensured its constant presence in people's lives. During the summer of 1919, Polly Wright and Annie Griffiths attended an event on 'Fairy Life' organized by the Bradford branch of the Theosophical Society, at which they mentioned their daughters' fairy photographs. In turn, Edward L. Gardner, president of the Blavatsky Lodge of the Theosophical Society in London, learnt of these photographs. The Bradford branch passed on copies, whereupon Gardner contacted the Wrights and asked them to make available the original negatives, so that he could check them. The Wrights duly sent off the negatives and Gardner consulted a specialist in trick photography, who confirmed that the plates had not been tampered with after exposure.

Encouraged by this certificate of authenticity, Gardner began to use the photographs at the public lectures that made up most of his work for the Theosophical Society. In this way the photographs came to the attention of Sir Arthur Conan Doyle, a writer whose name remains – as mentioned above – synonymous with rational analysis, thanks to his famous fictional detective. But this is only one facet of his complex personality. As we noted in Chapter 5, his uncle, Richard Doyle, was one of the leading fairy painters of the Victorian Age, while his father, Charles Altamont Doyle, spent much of his life in psychiatric institutions, where he made drawings of the fairies that visited him there. Scholars have suggested that one of the reasons for Sir Arthur's enthusiastic interest in the Cottingley fairy photographs may have lain in his own family history and in his desire to provide posthumous justification for his father's visions. But he also had a second, no less tragic, reason for taking an interest in the world of the supernatural: he had lost his own son in the First World War, and so had a highly personal reason for his intense commitment to the spiritualist movement, which sought to use pseudo-scientific means to prove the reality of life after death. In spiritualist circles there was also a fascination with the phenomenon of fairies, and it was the editor of the spiritualist journal *Light* who drew Conan Doyle's attention to the photographs of the Cottingley fairies.

Once contact had been established between Conan Doyle and Edward Gardner, a close (if somewhat one-sided) collaboration developed between them: although Gardner undertook most of the research, the publications that resulted from their work together all appeared under Conan Doyle's name alone. Gardner interviewed Elsie and Frances and collected the material not only for Conan Doyle's editorial in the December 1920 issue of *The Strand*, but also for a whole series of subsequent publications. But both men anticipated that any publication of the Cottingley fairy photographs would inevitably lead to calls for further photographic proof, and so Gardner provided both Elsie and Frances with cameras with which to take more fairy photographs, and in that way pre-empt any subsequent criticism. During the summer of 1920, the two girls did indeed use these cameras to take three more photographs of fairies. These showed a winged fairy offering flowers to Elsie; several fairies sunbathing in a bower woven from grass; and Frances with a fairy seen leaping through the air (Illus. 23).

Even Conan Doyle's first article in the Christmas issue of *The Strand* in 1920 sold out within a matter of days. A further series of articles elicited a response ranging from enthusiasm to embarrassment and led to a lively debate in the daily papers. Two years later, Conan Doyle published his first full-length book on the Cottingley fairy photographs, *The Coming of the Fairies*, the first edition of which sold out practically overnight. It was only the first in a long series of publications on the photographs of Elsie Wright and Frances Griffiths – photographs that have become known as the 'Cottingley photographs' and that are now the most famous of all photographs of fairies. As a classic of fairy literature, *The Coming of the Fairies* is representative of many of the ideas that became established in esoteric circles in the early twentieth century. It is also a text that directly or indirectly was later to prove enormously influential.

23. 'Frances and the Leaping Fairy', August 1920.

The Coming of the Fairies presents the Cottingley photographs as an 'epoch-making' event that afforded quasi-scientific proof of the existence of an entire world that, until then, most people had doubted existed at all. Here Conan Doyle saw the potential for casting a spell on the world all over again, and for calling into question the materialistic foundations of his age:

> The thought of them [i.e. these fairies], even when unseen, will add a charm to every brook and valley and give romantic interest to every country walk. The recognition of their existence will jolt the material twentieth-century mind out of its heavy ruts in the mud, and will make it admit that there is a glamour and a mystery to life.[4]

Quite apart from the idea underpinning the book as a whole – that magic and mystery might return to the world – Conan Doyle also put forward a series of theories relating to a far more specific question: what exactly are fairies? These theories go into such depth and such detail that, given the relative lack of any empirical material relating to 'real fairies', contemporary readers were bound to find them unconvincing. Here Conan Doyle is happy to leave the theosophist Edward Gardner to do the talking and explain the nature of elves and fairies within the context of theosophical ideas.

Entirely typical of the theories proposed in *The Coming of the Fairies* is a curious mixture of scientific terminology and esoteric ideas: the abilities of mediums and seers, for example, are naturally regarded as real. These ideas are put forward in a tone of utter conviction. Time and again, Conan Doyle develops a theory of fairies as beings that 'vibrate on a different level' from humans. It is one that he seeks to illustrate with reference to the visible colour spectrum. The human eye can see only a part of the colour spectrum of light, but this spectrum continues on either side of the section that is visible to us humans. It is the same with creatures like fairies: they, too, are material realities, but their materiality operates on a level of the 'spectrum of vibration' that lies beyond the area that we ourselves can normally see. Only certain people – notably children before the onset of puberty – have the ability to see this range of 'vibrations'. A somewhat different formulation, albeit one that on its most basic level is fundamentally the same, is found in the chapter headed 'The Theosophic View of Fairies', which relies for the most part on Gardner's notes. Here we learn that fairies may be physical, material beings, but their materiality is so thin that they are not normally perceptible to the human senses. Or, as Gardner puts it: 'Fairies use bodies of a density that we should describe, in non-technical language, as of a lighter than gaseous nature.'[5] Yet even here Gardner avails himself of a pseudo-scientific language to describe an occult object, except that on this occasion the occult is rationalized not as a 'vibration' but as 'gaseous'.

As represented by Gardner, the theosophical view of fairies is not as 'higher' beings. Indeed, exactly the opposite is the case. For a theosophist like Gardner, fairies are part of a natural evolutionary process, but they are not part of the same branch of evolution as mammals (including humankind), being akin, rather, to winged insects:

> Allied to the *lepidoptera*, or butterfly genus, of our familiar acquaintance rather than to the mammalian line, they partake of certain characteristics that are obvious. There is little or no mentality awake – simply a gladsome, irresponsible joyousness of life that is abundantly in evidence in their enchanting abandon.[6]

These insect-like fairies may have little conscious awareness, but they have a function in relation to the life of plants:

> The function of the nature spirit of woodland, meadow, and garden, indeed in connection with vegetation generally, is to furnish the vital connecting link between the stimulating energy of the sun and the raw material of the form. That growth of a plant which we regard as the customary and inevitable result of associating the three factors of sun, seed, and soil would never take place if the fairy builders were absent.[7]

Here fairies are seen as a workforce operating in the world of plants and responsible for the fact that natural processes can function at all. Gardner even goes so far as to differentiate between different kinds of fairy, each of which is responsible for individual parts of the plant's development: one group is in charge of the growth and organization of cells, another for the development of the underground system of roots, and a third for colouring the petals of the flowers. Gardner uses the word 'magnetic' to describe the way in which these fairies carry out their work within the individual plant — another example of his use of a pseudo-scientific term. Normally, he goes on, fairies would have no clear form, but consist of small, hazy and somewhat luminous clouds of colour with a brighter spark-like nucleus. These clouds assume human form only occasionally, and then perhaps only under the influence of human thought. Their wings are not used for flying but are a result of the streaming motion of their cloud-like bodies. The lower nature spirits are incapable of speaking, and it is possible to communicate with them — as with domestic animals — only through gestures and tone of voice. Human relations with them are similar to those with young dogs and cats and birds.

Only the higher nature spirits have any mental capabilities and can speak, and yet their communications with the world of humans are anything but positive, as they resent the fact that humans are destroying the environment and polluting the atmosphere.

The Cottingley photographs and the resultant public debate have continued to resonate right down to the present day. Conan Doyle made himself look ridiculous with his defence of these photographs, and yet he was still publishing texts on the subject until shortly before his death in 1930 and appears to have believed they were genuine right up until the end. Not until the 1980s did the now elderly Elsie Wright and Frances Griffiths admit that they themselves had created the fairy figures that they had photographed in 1917 and 1920. Yet even then, Frances's admission was accompanied by the qualification that her final photograph showed genuine fairies and by her insistence that she herself had repeatedly seen fairies by the beck in Cottingley.

Up until the time of Elsie's and Frances's 'confession', the Cottingley photographs remained the subject of a whole series of book-length studies and television documentaries, which meant that hardly anyone in Great Britain – and even interested parties much further afield – was unaware of their purported existence. Even after the two women's partial confession, the Cottingley fairies retained their abiding fascination. In 1992, for example, Steve Szilagyi published a novel titled *Photographing Fairies* that was turned into a film in 1997 with Ben Kingsley in one of the leading roles. The director was Nick Willing. Another film released in 1997 was Charles Sturridge's *Fairy Tale: A True Story*, with Peter O'Toole as Conan Doyle. More recently there have been two novels, *The Cottingley Secret* (2017) by Hazel Gaynor and *The Cottingley Cuckoo* (2021) by Alison Littlewood, who publishes under the name of A.J.

Elwood. There appears to be no end in sight to the fascination with fairies triggered by Elsie Wright and Frances Griffiths.

In short, the Cottingley fairies had an extraordinary impact on the public perception of elves and fairies – an impact that went hand in hand, conversely, with a catastrophic devaluation of the standing of these creatures: the reader will recall that the theosophical fairies of *The Coming of the Fairies* combined the size and evolutionary pedigree of insects with the intelligence of a puppy. As a result, this high point in public awareness of fairies also marked a low point in contemporaries' perception of them. Rarely before had fairies been so tiny. Writers on the subject have tended, therefore, to blame the Cottingley fairies for the decline in the stature of fairies in general after this time. Post-Cottingley, these writers argue that elves and fairies are no longer a legitimate object of scientific enquiry and cultivated interest. But there is life in the old fairies yet.

The Fairy Investigation Society

The Roaring Twenties were a good time for elves and fairies, who featured in an astonishing number of lasting classics of fairy literature during that decade. I have already mentioned the publication of the stage version of Barrie's *Peter Pan* (1928), Sir Arthur Conan Doyle's book about the Cottingley fairies (1922) and important works by Lady Gregory and W.B. Yeats; but no list would be complete without the novel *The King of Elfland's Daughter* (1924) by Lord Dunsany, one of the founding fathers of modern fantasy fiction, and *Lud-in-the-Mist* (1926), arguably one of the most enchanting literary treatments of fairyland in the early twentieth century, whose author, Hope Mirrlees, was the lifelong companion of the eminent mythographer Jane Ellen Harrison. In 1923, the painter Cicely Mary Barker published the first volume in her series of books on 'flower fairies', *Flower Fairies of the Spring*, in which she combined botanically correct depictions of plants with tiny winged fairies, modelled on children from the nursery school that was run by her sister (Illus. 24). Here the folktale figures who once stole children have themselves become children. These illustrations were accompanied by short poems that provided basic information about the flowers in question, information tailored to the needs of children. With its combination of imagination, innocence and lessons in natural history, Barker's eight-volume series of *Flower Fairies* books proved one of the most successful products of fairy art and has remained in print to the present day.

In the 1920s, elves and fairies were still a respectable subject for the art and literature of the upper middle classes. It is worth stressing that all the aforementioned milestones in the history of art and literature about fairies were the work of members of the upper middle classes and even the aristocracy of the British Isles, not of the common people: neither the rural peasant population nor the working classes played any part in these developments.

One member of the artistic circles who dominated this particular branch of the cultural history of elves and fairies was Bernard Sleigh (1872–1954), who made a name for himself more especially with his wood engravings, book illustrations and murals, and his work as a stained-glass artist. In each of these different mediums he repeatedly returned to the theme of fairies. Starting in 1917, he published several editions of a printed wall map of fairyland, *An Ancient Mappe of Fairyland*, that appeared in several sizes, one of the larger ones measuring 47 x 178cm (18.5 x 70 inches) – so big that it must have dominated any room in which it was displayed. Within a single panorama, Sleigh's map brings together a

24. 'The Speedwell Fairy', from Cicely Mary Barker's
Flower Fairies of the Spring (1923).

veritable kaleidoscope of fairytale figures and stories: among the figures depicted are not only slender-limbed fairies with dragonfly wings, but also brownies, an elfin town, characters from *Alice in Wonderland* and Atlantis and, finally, the Holy Grail. In 1920, he collaborated with Ivy Anne Ellis on a 'Faery Calendar' featuring woodcuts of fairies appropriate to each of the seasons and accompanied by little poems. But Sleigh's most influential engagement with the world of elves and fairies was a work that stands apart from his usual field of endeavour as a visual artist: the novel *The Gates of Horn: Being Sundry Records from the Proceedings of the Society for the Investigation of Faery Fact and Fallacy* (1926).

The book's title alludes to a passage in Homer's *Odyssey*, where Penelope explains to her husband that dreams come to us through two gates – one of horn, the other of ivory: true dreams come through the gates of horn, false ones through those of ivory. This allusion to Homer's epic poem is programmatical, making it clear from the outset that the dreams that Sleigh is describing are – at least in his own eyes – true. This literary conceit is continued in the subtitle of the novel, which describes a society of amateur scholars whose aim it is to prove the existence of fairies by scientific means. Sleigh explains that the impetus to found this Faery Investigation Society was Sir Arthur Conan Doyle's *The Coming of the Fairies*, and that its members met not only to celebrate Celtic festivals, but also to place a bowl of cream in the garden for the fairies and to discuss reports on actual encounters with fairy folk. The bulk of the book is a collection of largely unconnected short stories, each of which purports to tell of a genuine meeting between humans and fairies. Each account is presented as a record gleaned from the archives of the Faery Investigation Society.

Even in themselves, these accounts are of considerable interest in terms of the history of narratives about elves and fairies. They unfold not only in the rural environment traditionally associated with fairies, but also in urban settings, contemporary slums and a tramcar, making *The Gates of Horn* a remarkable early precursor of the urban fantasy novel that was to establish itself as a popular genre at the end of the twentieth century. Sleigh's novel perpetuated the metaphorical use of scientific terms such as 'vibrations' and 'wavelengths' that Conan Doyle had already used in *The Coming of the Fairies*. It also showed the way forward in its emphasis on the link between fairies and a new longing for a systematic kind of conservationism. The idea that fairies held humans responsible for polluting the planet had already been mentioned in *The Coming of the Fairies*, of course; but as the historian Simon Young has emphasized, no work of literature had previously forged such a powerful link between fairies and conservationism as *The Gates of Horn*.[8] Even the poem headed 'Faery Faith' that Sleigh wrote by way of a preface to the volume describes the grief felt by fairies at the human destruction of the environment, which is presented as a key element in their view of the modern world:

> Still do they wander here
> Disconsolate upon this earth we spoil,
> With wistful eyes that peer
> Upon the ugliness of mortal toil.[9]

The individual tales that follow on from this introduction are presented as actual accounts of genuine encounters with fairies. There is nothing unusual, of course, about a novel claiming that it is based on true events, but in constructing his narrative world Sleigh used this idea so skilfully that no fewer than two contemporary reviewers asked if the Faery Investigation Society that he described actually existed. Their question was to prove prophetic.

One of the readers of *The Gates of Horn* was Captain Quentin Charles Alexander Craufurd (1875–1957), a man whom no one could claim did not have both feet planted firmly on the ground: as an officer in the Royal Navy he had spent much of the First World War as commander of the destroyer HMS *Rother*, and as a scientist and engineer he was a pioneer of wireless technology. But Craufurd also had a pronounced interest in spiritualism and the supernatural in general, and after reading *The Gates of Horn* he contacted Sleigh. By 1927, the two men had founded an actual Fairy

Investigation Society in London: in a certain sense, then, it was a case of life imitating art.

The interwar history of the Fairy Investigation Society is poorly documented and therefore difficult to reconstruct. Craufurd later wrote that practically all its early records were destroyed by enemy action during the Second World War, when London was heavily bombed. Its members shared a common interest in spiritualism and theosophy, and came from a philosophical background similar to that of Gardner and Conan Doyle. Within this circle, elves and fairies were typically described as 'nature spirits' and as 'elemental beings'. This had little to do with the traditional narratives of the rural population, but that population was never part of the clientele of the Fairy Investigation Society, whose members prior to the Second World War came, for the most part, from the upper middle class and the aristocracy, and from the world of art.

The oldest surviving membership lists from the 1950s include the names of Hugh Dowding, air chief marshal in the Second World War; Major Wellesley Tudor Pole, who founded the Chalice Well Trust at Glastonbury and played a key role in the quest for the Holy Grail in Great Britain; the aforementioned Edward L. Gardner; the surrealist artist Ithell Colquhoun; and even Walt Disney. In general, however, the elitist aspect of the Fairy Investigation Society was less pronounced after the Second World War. By 1950, if not before, its secretary was Marjorie Thelma Johnson (1911–2011), making her effectively the society's director and, as such, its driving force.

Marjorie Johnson did not belong to the social circles that had dominated the Fairy Investigation Society prior to the Second World War, but was born in Nottingham, where she spent the whole of her life. She published her first article in a British literary magazine when she was twenty-five, and in it described how, as a child of seven or eight, she had seen an elf in her room. Visions of fairies accompanied her throughout the rest of her long life – she lived to be one hundred. Collecting encounters with fairies was one of her main interests. The members of the Fairy Investigation Society allowed her to assemble what is probably the largest collection of such records from the middle of the twentieth century, running to around four hundred reports of sightings. But it was one of the tragedies of her life that this collection never appeared in print in English during her lifetime. It took decades to find a publisher for these voluminous records. Ironically, the volume finally appeared in German in 2000 under the imprint of Aquamarin Verlag in Grafing, Bavaria. Its German title was *Naturgeister: Wahre Erlebnisse mit Elfen und Zwergen* (*Nature Spirits: True Experiences with Elves and Dwarves*). An Italian translation of the German appeared four years later under the title *Il popolo del bosco* (*The People of the Woods*). Titled *Seeing Fairies*, the English original was not published until 2014, three years after Marjorie Johnson's death. By then, the Fairy Investigation Society had vanished with barely a trace.

This collection of sightings of fairies collected by Marjorie Johnson and the Fairy Investigation Society has outlived its creators and remains an exceptional source of subjectively real encounters with elves and fairies. As Simon Young has emphasized, it is one of our most important sources in terms of the way in which our picture of fairies developed in the twentieth century.[10] Anyone who reads about these alleged sightings of fairies will be struck by at least three things. First, the fairies in *Seeing Fairies* have wings, setting them apart from the reports of sightings in the nineteenth century and earlier, when fairies had wings only in artistic representations of them, but not yet in reports of actual encounters: the images produced in artistic circles in the nineteenth century were not taken over into the empirical world of a wider audience until the twentieth century. Second, the fairies of *Seeing Fairies* are always an intrinsic part of 'nature': traditional rural fairies and the fairies of nineteenth-century art may exist in a rural setting, but they are far from being 'nature spirits' concerned with nature as such and with its survival. The view of fairies as the architects of nature and as environmental activists from the otherworld that was developed in books such as *The Coming of the Fairies* and *The Gates of Horn* did not reach a broader cross-section of the population until the middle of the twentieth century. The third innovation is that these modern fairies are benign and do not pose a threat. The fairies of traditional folk belief represented an incalculable danger, and even the fairies of Victorian fairy painters such as John Anster Fitzgerald and Richard Doyle had at least a weakness for animal cruelty. The sightings of fairies collected by Marjorie Johnson, on the other hand, are at worst mildly unsettling, but never dangerous. As a rule, her fairies are small, delicate and nice.

A few examples may serve to illustrate the way in which the 'new fairies' that represented the new suburban folklore of the twentieth century were perceived. Many of Johnson's accounts come from letters that she received:

> From Bulawayo, Southern Rhodesia, Mr. Stuart W. Wright wrote that many years ago he had a little daughter who used to chase fairies from flower to flower. She would run excitedly from one part of the garden to the other, calling to her father to look at some particular flower on which a fairy was perching for the moment, and she could

not understand why he was unable to see any of these sprites.[11]

No less dramatic is a report from the south coast of England:

> Writing about the flower fairies in her garden, Mrs. D. Goddard, of Hampshire, wrote: 'They are so tiny and luminous that the very air seems lighter as I sense them. They seem to me to have slight little bodies with gossamer wings. I feel they pass on some of their lovely colours to the flowers as they open, as one would paint the hues on a painting. They are too wonderful to describe in our language because the brilliance of their presence makes physical things only half as beautiful in comparison. I feel they play an important part in God's creation.'[12]

Or take this description of a front garden in Scotland:

> Mrs. Maybelle Gillespie's son, Thomas, used to see fairies in his native Galloway, mostly near the house and in the garden. Especially he liked the 'lady fairies', as he called them; and the way the fairies help to show the birds where to get food and berries in wintry weather.[13]

These fairies paint flowers and feed little birds. They are no longer the powerful, menacing figures from traditional folk beliefs or from the ballads of the early modern period. They do not even have the spirited jealousy of Barrie's original Tinker Bell or the ambivalence of Peter Pan. The evidence presented in *Seeing Fairies* represents a trivialization of fairies, a reductive process that renders them harmless in a way prefigured in *The Coming of the Fairies*. They have now been reduced to a twee personification of plant life and of the pretty little things of nature. Even while this process was taking place, a number of contemporaries saw it as the ultimate debasement of beings from the otherworld who had once been so immensely powerful. Protests were not long in coming.

CHAPTER 7

ELVES AND FAIRIES AFTER THE SECOND WORLD WAR

International Popular Culture between Playing with History, Environmental Protection and the New Age

Once it had been established by the middle of the twentieth century that fairies were tiny creatures with insect wings, the mythology associated with them could sink no further: fairies were infantilized and robbed of their original status as some of the most powerful figures in the otherworld. At about the time that this new picture of fairies was acquiring canonical status, however, a countermovement was getting under way with the work of J.R.R. Tolkien, restoring something of the old ambiguity to elves and fairies and giving them back some of their traditional status. True, this new attitude was no longer a part of a belief system rooted in the common people, but involved a largely urban reading public. This chapter will examine the changes brought about by Tolkien and look in greater detail at some of the more important aspects of the treatment of elves and fairies from the middle of the twentieth century onwards. At the end I shall return to Iceland, an island not untouched by international developments in our picture of elves and fairies. Here, more especially in the urban environment of the capital Reykjavík, traditional Icelandic ideas have largely been overlaid by the international image of fairies that came to predominate in the later twentieth century. This development had nothing to do with Tolkien, however, but involved the very trivialization of fairies that Tolkien had sought so hard to resist.

J.R.R. Tolkien's 'On Fairy-stories' and the Renaissance of Medieval Elves

John Ronald Reuel Tolkien (1892–1973) was the single most influential figure in the history of fantasy fiction in the twentieth century. An academic by profession, he researched the languages and literatures of northwestern Europe in the Middle Ages, more especially Old English and Old Norse. From 1925 until his retirement in 1959, he taught at Oxford University. His two main literary works were *The Hobbit* (1937) and *The Lord of the Rings*, which was first published in three volumes in 1954–55. With them he pioneered the genre of modern fantasy fiction. Both were the result of considerable reflection. In his essay 'On Fairy-stories' of 1947, Tolkien set out a detailed programme of his work as a writer; but he also explored the ways in which ideas about fairies can be used in literature to their greatest effect – or not, as the case may be. In particular, he took aim at the tiny winged creatures with insect-like features that had found a place for themselves in English literature since Shakespeare's day. In discussing these fairies, he did not mince his words, but let his readers know in no uncertain terms that he had no time for 'that long line of flower-fairies and fluttering sprites with antennae that I so disliked as a child, and which my children in their turn detested'.[1] In taking this stance and dismissing flower fairies as literary constructs, Tolkien was aligning himself with the folklorist Andrew Lang, who as long ago as 1910 had written in the introduction to his collection of fairytales, *The Lilac Fairy Book*:

> But the three hundred and sixty-five authors who try to write new fairy tales are very tiresome. They always begin with a little boy or girl who goes out and meets the fairies of polyanthuses and gardenias and apple blossoms. 'Flowers and fruits, and other winged things.' These fairies try to be funny, and fail; or they try to preach, and succeed ... At the end, the little boy or girl wakes up and finds that he has been dreaming. Such are the new fairy stories. May we be preserved from all the sort of them![2]

Tolkien responded proactively to this critique of the new fairies with their diminutive stature and insect-like wings. As a medievalist, he was as familiar with the elves of medieval Iceland and Ireland discussed in Chapters 1 and 2 as he was with Arthurian literature and the ballads of the early modern period that I examined in Chapter 3. And it was from these sources that he drew the models for the elves in his own literary writings.

Tolkien's profound knowledge of medieval literature opened up a treasure-house of themes of encyclopaedic breadth, allowing him a chance to borrow the most varied ideas that he then welded together in a spirit of great ingenuity. I mentioned the Old Norse *Alvíssmál* in Chapter 1: this is the poem that almost certainly provided the inspiration for Tolkien's decision to create different languages for his Elves, Dwarves and Men. In much the same way, the skilful elf smith Vǫlundr in Old Norse literature presumably inspired the idea of Tolkien's Elves possessing superior skills as smiths. The distinction that the medieval Icelandic writer Snorri Sturluson draws between 'light-elves' (*ljósálfar*) and 'dark-elves' (*døkkálfar*) was reworked by Tolkien in *The Silmarillion*, where a contrast is drawn between Calaquendi ('Elves of the Light') and Moriquendi ('Elves of the Darkness'). The Elves' home in the cursed forest of Mirkwood in *The Hobbit* also reflects the traditional setting for encounters with fairies in Arthurian texts that I discussed in Chapter 3 in the context of the Old French *Lai de Lanval* and *Lai de Guingamor*, where characters who enter a forest are more than likely to run into a female fairy.

Tolkien also used motifs from otherworld literature from ancient Ireland. In Chapter Nine of Book Two of *The Lord of the Rings*, Frodo, Legolas and Aragorn discuss the way in which time passes differently for Elves than it does for humans: during the time that they spend in the Elves' woodland realm of Lothlórien, time passes more quickly than they realize. Even if only in a less extreme form, the way in which time passes here recalls a motif found throughout Irish literature, where the passage of time in the otherworld is unrelated to that of the human world. No one who enters the Irish otherworld knows how much time has elapsed in the human world when he or she returns home. A man who in *Bran's Sea Voyage* places his foot on the ground after spending some time in the otherworld crumbles at once into dust.

One motif that recurs again and again in Tolkien's writings, and that is explored in greater detail in *The Silmarillion*, is the close relationship between his Elves and a land in the West, beyond the sea – a land that provides the Elves of Middle-earth with their final place of refuge. This land is especially important at the end of *The Lord of the Rings*, where, in the very last chapter of all ('The Grey Havens') Elrond and Galadriel take Frodo and Bilbo with them to the West, when they leave Middle-earth. This reflects the Irish motif that the otherworld was located on an island in the West, beyond the sea, and it also mirrors the basic plot of Old Irish texts such as *Connle's Journey to the Otherworld* and *Bran's Sea Voyage*, which are among the oldest surviving examples of Irish literature. Like Frodo and Bilbo, the heroes of these two texts are ultimately spirited away to the fairy world beyond the sea, where it appears that they lead blissful lives and never die (see Chapter 2).

The multilayered manner in which Tolkien weaves together the strands of other historical narratives to create the world of Middle-earth even extends to the way in which he integrates historical prejudices. When, shortly after their visit to Lothlórien, Aragorn, Gimli and Legolas set off in pursuit of the Orcs that have abducted Merry and Pippin, they surprise a unit of Riders of Rohan. Their commander Éomer is more than mistrustful:

'Are you elvish folk?'

'No,' said Aragorn. 'One only of us is an Elf, Legolas from the Woodland Realm in distant Mirkwood. But we have passed through Lothlórien, and the gifts and favour of the Lady go with us.'

The Rider looked at them with renewed wonder, but his eyes hardened. 'Then there is a Lady in the Golden Wood, as old tales tell!' he said. 'Few escape her nets, they say. These are strange days! But if you have her favour, then you also are net-weavers and sorcerers, maybe.'[3]

So offended is Gimli at Éomer's words that the two of them almost come to blows. But Éomer's fear of the power of the Lady of Lothlórien harks back to historical models: after all, the female fairies of the Breton *lais* and of many of the texts of medieval Arthurian literature are precisely what Éomer is afraid of: powerful sorceresses in a wood from which a knight who has lost his way there can never escape. Even the suspicion that the companions who enjoy the favour of the Lady of the Golden Wood may themselves be sorcerers reflects a traditional narrative motif: after the years that Thomas the Rhymer spent with the Queen of Elfland, he returned as a prophet; and in Scottish witch trials the accused repeatedly claimed that they had learnt their magic practices from fairy folk. If a person returns from the land of elves and fairies, then he or she is suspected of possessing similar magic powers. Here Tolkien performs a kind of literary backward somersault, not only by fashioning his own Elves in the image of historical elves, but also by picking up the motif whereby humans were historically afraid of these elves. In Tolkien's case, of course, this insinuation is emphatically rejected by Gimli.

Quite apart from their intrinsic interest as stories told with great imagination and invested with palpable tension, Tolkien's writings acquire an additional layer of charm by virtue of the wealth of their historical allusions. Their author has achieved nothing less than a literary reworking of several centuries of the cultural history of elves and fairies. Few other authors have been as successful as Tolkien in reworking a comparable repository of cultural and historical allusions and applying them to a literary work about elves.

Elves and Fairies after Tolkien: Between Historical Subject Matter, Social Criticism and Ecological Concerns

The extraordinary success of *The Hobbit* and *The Lord of the Rings* turned Tolkien into one of the fathers of modern fantasy fiction, and his influence can be felt in the works of many writers – as well as in their depiction of elves – right down to the present day. Some of the best-known examples are Terry Brooks with his *Shannara* series of novels starting in 1977; Andrzej Sapkowski with his six-volume series *The Witcher*, first published in Polish beginning in 1994, with an English translation appearing from 2007 onwards; Bernhard Hennen, whose five-volume series *Drachenelfen* (*Dragon Elves*) was published between 2011 and 2016; and Wolfgang Hohlbein, whose *Chroniken der Elfen* (*Chronicles of the Elves*) appeared in three volumes between 2009 and 2011.

Among those of Tolkien's methods that were to leave their mark on many later literary reworkings of tales of elves and fairies, one of the most important was his recourse to historical models. Indeed, his influence may be said to have played an essential role in the fact that many of the fantasy novels of the last few decades are adaptations of historical narratives.

Among the tales on which these reworkings have been based, two in particular stand out: namely, the Scottish ballads of Tam Lin and Thomas the Rhymer discussed in Chapter 3. Since the Second World War these two ballads have been adapted for literally dozens of fantasy novels. One of them is Ellen Kushner's novel *Thomas the Rhymer*, which was first published in 1990 and which won the Mythopoeic Award and the World Fantasy Award the following year. These are among the most prestigious prizes in the realm of fantasy fiction. In her basic narrative structure, Kushner has stuck closely to the outlines of the ballad. Her Thomas is an itinerant bard who earns his daily bread by performing his songs at the courts of the gentry and accompanying them on his harp. He meets the Queen of Elfland by the Eildon Tree. In keeping with tradition, she is riding on a white horse. He addresses her as the Queen of Heaven and, ignoring her warning about the consequences, becomes her lover and spends the next seven years in the fairy world. When he returns to the world of humans, it is as a changed person and as a seer who can speak only the truth.

But, unlike the ballad, Kushner's novel describes only the otherworldly aspect of the action from Thomas's point of view. The other three sections of the four-part novel tell the story from the standpoint of Gavin the crofter and his wife Meg, and from that of Elspeth, who is initially a young woman. Thomas knows all three of them both before and after his time with the Fairy Queen, and the focus of the story lies less on any fantasy elements than on Thomas's developing character. Only through his suffering in the otherworld does Thomas learn to empathize with the fates of others. His disappearance causes Elspeth immense suffering and leaves her feeling profoundly hurt. Despite this, Thomas and Elspeth marry when he returns home. They spend a long life together, at the end of which Elspeth nurses Thomas through his final illness, even though she is never able to forget the pain that he caused her during her youth. In short, Kushner uses the historical subject matter as the starting point for a study in human development that explores the highs and lows and the challenges that all of us face in our interpersonal relationships.

In the twentieth and twenty-first centuries, historical subjects have been used not only in the form of literary adaptations of much older tales, but also as the basis of historical novels in the narrower sense of the term – that is, in the form of a literary reworking of historical events. A recent example of this type of novel is *The Good People* (2016) by the Australian writer Hannah Kent. This novel, too, deals with the abduction of humans by fairies, but it remains entirely within the realm of what is historically possible and verifiable.

It is set in rural Ireland in 1825. One of its leading figures is Nóra Leahy, a woman ill used by fate. Her daughter died when she was still very young, leaving behind her a severely handicapped child whom Nóra herself has to care for. When Nóra's husband dies as well, her situation becomes unbearable. Poverty, hopelessness and the absence of all other forms of support finally persuade Nóra to turn for help to a traditional healer and 'cunning woman', Nance Roche, also known as 'Nance of the Fairies'. Nance lives on her own in a little cottage by a fairy tree and helps people whom the Church and doctors have abandoned. On the basis of her own belief system, Nance is convinced that the child is a changeling and wants to help in the only way that she knows how: by driving out the changeling and trying to persuade the fairies to restore Nóra's true grandchild. But instead of saving the child, her efforts lead only to tragedy.

Hannah Kent's novel is a fictional reworking of events that actually took place, leading to a trial in 1826 that is recorded in court documents. According to these records, the Tralee Assizes in County Kerry tried the case of an old woman called Anne or Nance Roche, who was charged with having drowned a handicapped child in a river. Her defence counsel argued that it was never Anne's (or Nance's) intention to kill the child, but only to heal it by driving out the fairy that was inhabiting its body. On this basis, the court acquitted her (as other courts, too, tended to do in such circumstances). Kent used this material to turn her novel into a study of the way in which humans deal with unbearable suffering and to discuss the social constraints, the lack of support by the authorities, especially the Church, and the clash of conflicting world-views in Irish society in the early nineteenth century. One of her literary achievements lies in her sympathetic exploration both of the good intentions of all the people caught up in the death of the child and of the traditional system of 'superstitious' beliefs – a system that, in the face of indifference on the part of the authorities, and of neglect and arrogance on the part of the Church, offered support to the poorest members of society (without, of course, putting them in any position to overcome the brutal realities of their lives in the here and now).

But the fairy literature of the twentieth and twenty-first centuries has in general produced more works of fantasy fiction than historical novels. Adumbrated by early examples such as Bernard Sleigh's *The Gates of Horn*, it witnessed a new development in the final third of the twentieth century, with the rise of 'urban fantasy' as a significant subgenre. These works are set in urban areas, often in cities that represent an alternative version of the present day and that are invaded by elements of fantasy.

An important role in the emergence of this form of fantasy fiction was played by the American writer Emma Bull (1954–), whose first novel, *War for the Oaks* (1987), won the Locus Award and was nominated for a long list of other literary prizes. Bull takes up a motif that is occasionally mentioned in Scottish folktales from the late nineteenth century onwards: the existence of two opposing royal courts of fairies, the Seelie Court and the Unseelie Court, the first of which is blessed, while the second is 'unblessed'. To put it crudely, these are the courts of good and wicked fairies. These opposing courts are nowhere mentioned in any of the older texts that discuss ideas about fairies, such as the ballads examined in Chapter 3 or Robert Kirk's *The Secret Commonwealth*, and do not appear to have played much of a role in later Scottish folktales either. But it did not take long for the literary potential of the idea of such a powerful dualism within the fairy world to be recognized by the writers of fantasy fiction, with the result that the terms Seelie and Unseelie Court are found much more frequently in modern fantasy fiction than was ever the case in traditional Scottish folktales. Bull's stroke of genius in *War for the Oaks* consisted in locating the conflict between the Seelie Court and the Unseelie Court at the very heart of Minneapolis, where the guitarist Eddi McCandry, previously unaware of the existence of any world beyond her own, is drawn into the conflict between the two courts. If she is to survive, she needs to learn very quickly that there are more things in heaven and earth than she could ever have dreamt of. In the course of the lively narrative, which is not without humour, she develops into a woman able to get a grip not just on her guitar, but also on the fairy world.

A further element that is frequently found in the treatment of elves and fairies in modern fantasy fiction is the use of postmodern irony: the otherworld is not necessarily taken seriously, but is often used for comic effect. The most successful and best-known exponent of fantasy fiction as a vehicle for comedy is arguably the British writer Terry Pratchett (1948–2015), many of whose forty-one *Discworld* novels feature fairies and elves, most notably in *Lords and Ladies* (1992) and *The Shepherd's Crown* (2015). Both novels deal, in essence, with the same underlying idea – one that implicitly turns on its head the picture of fairies that is found in many children's books, more especially those that include fairies of the 'flower fairy' variety: fairies are no longer cute, but are domineering, unfeeling and cruel. Humans have to be careful to ensure that the boundaries of their own world are secure and safe from attack. In both novels, fairies try to storm the human world, in the first case under their queen (the fairy king has no say in the matter), and in the second, under the command of a fairy lord who has dethroned his queen. Their aim is to be able to hunt in the human world and to play with human toys to their hearts' content. It is left to the witches to ensure that this attempt fails and that the invasion from the otherworld is driven back. In *Lords and Ladies*, they succeed in this endeavour under the leadership of the powerful witch Granny Weatherwax, while in *The Shepherd's Crown* they are led by her successor, Tiffany Aching. Pratchett tells this story with a permanent twinkle in his eye, in paragraph after paragraph mocking both his characters and his readers. In both novels it is the witches who save the world, functioning as antithetical counterparts to conventional heroic figures. The entire plot of *Lords and Ladies* may be read as a pastiche of Shakespeare's *A Midsummer Night's Dream*.

But despite their fondness for playing disrespectful literary games, the authors of many of these works also strike a sociocritical note, adapting their depiction of elves and fairies to suit modern social concerns. Under this heading comes the house elf Dobby in *Harry Potter and the Chamber of Secrets* (1998), the second novel in the *Harry Potter* series of books by the writer J.K. Rowling. In the world of Harry Potter, Dobby is a house elf, which is tantamount to being a slave with no rights: the Malfoy family treats him ruthlessly and with extreme brutality, but he still has to perform every task that the family demands of him. He does not even own any decent clothing, but wears only a dirty pillowcase that symbolizes his status as a slave, since house elves can obtain their freedom only if their masters give them a piece of clothing. In the course of the novel, Dobby makes Harry Potter's life a living hell through his well-meaning but botched attempts to protect him from the Malfoy family's insidious actions. Dobby worships Harry as a champion of the rights of those members of the world of magic who lack the most basic freedoms. In this world of magic, non-human creatures are systematically oppressed and exploited. Towards the end of the book, Harry manages to free Dobby by tricking Lucius Malfoy into giving him a sock by mistake.

With the character of Dobby the house elf, Rowling has drawn on and elaborated the traditional folktale figure of the brownie, his name recalling the word 'dobie' that is used in the North of England to describe a brownie with limited intellectual abilities. The word 'dobby' is also attested in Yorkshire and Lancashire to refer to a playful, brownie-like creature. Brownies are already mentioned in Robert Kirk's *The Secret Commonwealth* to describe a type of supernatural being that performs housework for a family during the night. These traditional brownies exist alongside the family that they help. They are under no compulsion, but carry out their duties willingly, often receiving milk, cream and particularly appetizing cakes by way of a reward. But the folktales repeatedly state that it is forbidden to give such gifts to a brownie directly. One branch of the tradition justifies this by stating that the brownie is a free creature that does not want to enter into a dependent relationship by accepting any kind of salary. These brownies embody a dream on the part of an overworked rural population that could never do all the work expected of them before the advent of modern machinery. At the same time, traditional brownies represented a warning that farmworkers should be well treated, since any form of abuse or lack of respect would cause the brownie to leave the farm without further ado, or worse, seek revenge, with sometimes drastic consequences. Rowling turns this traditionally helpful but independent creature into a downtrodden slave and places this character – and its sufferings – at the heart of her novel, turning the text into an indictment of exploitative power relations and a demand that such exploitation be resisted. That these concerns were important to Rowling is clear from *The Casual Vacancy* (2012), the first novel that she wrote after completing the *Harry Potter* series. Here the focus is entirely on contemporary social problems. Whether set in the real world or in that of fantasy fiction, Rowling's works can also be read as a vehicle for social criticism, the elves of her narrative world being adapted in such a way as to convey a socio-critical message.

But in recent decades, the novels that have taken the world of fairies as their starting point have seemed more interested in ecological, rather than social, questions. This was a trend that can already be traced back to Bernard Sleigh's *The Gates of Horn*, if not earlier, and is now very firmly established. A particularly impressive example of this trend is the novella *The Wild Wood* (1994) by the Canadian fantasy writer Charles de Lint (1951–), who won the World Fantasy Award in 2000. The novel is about a young painter called Eithnie, who retires to a remote cabin in the Canadian outback in the hope of finding inspiration. However, it slowly becomes clear that her sketches are increasingly, if unwittingly, portraying figures from the fairy world. Finally, she even establishes direct contact with the fairies who inhabit the Canadian outback that surrounds her cabin. Eithnie now learns that even here, in the apparently remote depths of the Canadian forests, the nature spirits are dying out. In turn, this results in a new awareness of the massive, universal effects of air pollution, acid rain (which played a prominent role in public debates in the 1990s), the extinction of entire species and the loss of unspoilt habitats. In de Lint's novella the gradual destruction of the environment affects not only the material world, but also the spirits of nature – and not just locally, but on a global scale. Eithnie merges with the world of these threatened nature spirits, and in the end even becomes the mother of a child – which is supposed both to free Eithnie from a past trauma and also to help in saving the fairy world. Above all, however, she comes to realize that where questions of environmental protection are concerned, even the smallest action can help; and that thanks to the 'butterfly effect', every ecological effort can contribute to healing the world.

A number of critics have argued that because of its tendency to preach, and because the depiction of ecological problems rarely rises above the commonplace, *The Wild Wood* is not one of de Lint's better books. But its very extremes are the best possible illustration of a broader trend that sets out from the conviction that there is a link between elves and fairies and the natural space that they inhabit, and that this leads in turn to a closer connection with the specific concerns of all who are keen to protect the environment.

Just how well established this link has now become is clear not least from the fact that it repeatedly appears in books whose primary focus is not the environment. A good example of this is the *Artemis Fowl* series of novels by the Irish writer Eoin Colfer (1965–). Even the first book in this series, which focuses on telling a thrilling adventure story with breathtaking action sequences, catapulted Colfer to the first ranks of writers working in the field of young adult fiction. In his *Artemis Fowl* novels, an underground world of elves, dwarves, centaurs and other fabulous beings exists alongside our own human world. This alternative world is extremely advanced from a technological standpoint: the magic of the fairies is complemented by a technological superiority that is normally found only in science fiction. Colfer's highly mechanized fairies have a tremendous aversion to every kind of environmental pollution – an aversion that may not be central to these stories, but which is mentioned in passing again and again. In his first *Artemis Fowl* novel from 2001, he describes the fairy Holly Short flying over the English Channel:

> Once over the Channel, Holly flew low, skipping over the white-crested waves. She called out to the dolphins and

they rose to the surface, leaping from the water to match her pace. She could see the pollution in them, bleaching their skin white and causing red sores on their backs. And although she smiled, her heart was breaking. Mud People had a lot to answer for.[4]

Colfer's exceptionally popular books are adventure novels, not works about the environment, but even the fairies of an adventure novel now have a well-developed awareness of environmental issues.

The affinities between fairies and conservationism have long been established outside the literature industry. In the course of her research into neo-pagan alternative religions, more especially in the English-speaking world, the anthropologist Sabina Magliocco has noted that the overwhelming majority of the five hundred individuals who formed the core of her study regarded fairies as particularly closely associated with nature. In this kind of 'esoteric' discourse, fairies and related beings serve to formulate the idea of a spiritual re-enchantment of the world of nature, and in that way motivate us to protect the environment. Here there is evidence of the widespread belief that – as in Charles de Lint's novel – the destruction of the environment is also harmful to the fairy world. Conversely, it is believed that fairies who are benevolent will benefit human agriculture. According to statements gathered in the 1970s, the Findhorn community, which still exists in the North of Scotland and is known, among other things, for its alternative spirituality, was able to grow vegetables in prodigious quantities thanks to the help of the local nature spirits.

Similar phenomena were investigated by Andy Letcher in the context of environmental activism at the end of the twentieth century. An alternative religious movement that emerged in Great Britain was 'eco-paganism', which evolved in the context of protests against the massive road-building programmes of the 1990s. It, too, used fairy mythology as an essential tool in formulating its own world-view and collective identity: in this context, fairies became the figureheads in attempts to resist infrastructure projects that were regarded as acts of despoliation on the grandest scale. Although the fairies were used in a primarily symbolic way, it remains a fact that many of the people involved in this protest movement believed in their actual existence, an astonishingly large number of them claiming to have had first-hand experience of the same. These encounters, they argued, signalled the fairies' support for their campaign, such support encouraging and legitimizing their protest actions. Some of these sightings took place under the influence of hallucinogenic mushrooms (although within the group of activists, this was not necessarily seen as invalidating the experiences). That this could also produce some curious results is illustrated by an incident described by Letcher that took place as part of a campaign against the Newbury Bypass in 1995/96, when an activist who had just drunk some mushroom tea met an elf in the woods and was told that his actions were wrong-headed and that he should leave at once. The man packed his bags and left the protest camp the very next day.

Back to Iceland: Iceland's 'Elves' Representative' and a New View of Elves

In the same year as the Newbury Bypass elf encounter, an incident took place in Germany that was to have unexpected repercussions for the perception of elves and fairies throughout the German-speaking world. Here, too, a road-building scheme played a role. In the New Year's Eve 1995 edition of the newspaper *Frankfurter Rundschau*, the journalist Wolfgang Müller published an interview with Erla Stefánsdóttir in which he spoke to her about her role in Icelandic public life and her sightings of elves and fairies. Here he called her the 'Elves' Representative of the City of Reykjavík's Urban Planning Department' – *Elfenbeauftragte* in German. No one was more surprised than Müller himself by the repercussions of his neologism, as the term *Elfenbeauftragte*, 'Elves' Representative', struck a chord with contemporary readers and even now, thirty years later, remains familiar in the German-speaking world. Indeed, the idea of such a figure has now become so entrenched in popular German culture that in 2016 the German television channel ARD broadcast a detective story set in Iceland, in which the 'Elves' Representative' was murdered.

It had simply been Müller's aim to find a word to describe the medium Erla Stefánsdóttir, who at that date was completely unknown in Germany. He intended the term to be apt and respectful. The link with the Reykjavík City Council came about because she had recently been asked by the local Tourist Board to design an elfin map of Hafnarfjörður, one of the towns that make up the metropolitan region of Reykjavík. It was a task that had suggested the delightful term 'Elves' Representative'. But it was a phrase that was taken up with such enthusiasm that Müller effectively created a new figure in the world of the German belief in elves and fairies: an official representative of elves on a remote island in the Far North. Professionally speaking, Erla Stefánsdóttir was in fact a piano teacher who worked as a medium and seer only in her spare time and never held an official post with any municipal authority.

Even in her first and hugely consequential interview, Erla Stefánsdóttir referred repeatedly to the subject of road-building that was exercising British environmental activists at this time. In particular, she referred to the famous – and still widely discussed – case of the Álfhólsvegur (Elf Hill Way) in Kópavogur, another urban community in the metropolitan region of Reykjavík. Here the road suddenly narrows to leave space for the 'Elf Hill' that gives the place its name. This hill is a low but striking rocky eminence, where Erla Stefánsdóttir claimed to have seen a large elfin settlement. Another example that she mentioned in her interview relates to the Eastfjords at the other end of the island: here it was said that two excavator shovels had broken when an attempt was made to remove elf stones that lay in the path of a planned road. In the end, the elf stones remained where they were and the road was rerouted.

Erla Stefánsdóttir was neither the first nor the last seer to play a prominent role in debates on the course to be followed by roads in Iceland. Back in the early 1970s, a man who claimed to be able to see elves was consulted about the building of an expressway in the vicinity of Reykjavík. After a series of accidents and rumours about elves living in a particular rock had left the workforce involved in the project not a little unsettled, the theosophist Zophanías Pétursson was consulted. He spoke to the elves who lived in the stone and finally gave the authorities the green light, after the elves had informed him that their rock could be moved to another site. However, the rock broke in two while it was being moved, and that same night a bulldozer ran over a pipeline carrying water to a nearby fish farm, resulting in the death of seventy thousand fry. In the 1990s, at least one of the workmen who had been involved in the project reported that his whole life had been a succession of misfortunes since then.

Later, in 2013, the case of another expressway hit the headlines across the world: it was due to be built through the

Gálgahraun lava field that was part of a conservation area. The plans to build the new road led to a legal dispute that dragged on for years. Protests were held on the site, from which the protestors were forcibly removed by the police, with several arrests being made. The bone of contention was not just the fact that this was a conservation area, but also that there was a rock formation here that was reputed to be an elf church and that lay in the path of the planned road. The road was finally built after the church had been relocated.

The 'Elves' Representative' was by no means alone in her views and her activism. What was unusual, however, was the way in which those views reached an international audience, and the detailed nature of her reflections. As well as the several elf maps that she drew for various towns and settlements and the incalculable number of interviews that she gave, she also wrote two books in which she expounded her vision of Iceland's elf community. Her autobiography, *Lífssýn mín*, appeared in 2003 and was followed in 2010 by a collection of stories about her encounters with the fairy folk, published under the title of *Örsögur*. This second title appeared in an English translation in 2010.

Here Erla Stefánsdóttir describes the elfin world in a systematic way that is based on the belief that there is an intrinsic link between elves and nature and the latter's 'inner life'. Hand in hand with this description goes a clear ecological interest. In her collection of stories *Örsögur*, for example, she wrote:

> We humans believe that the Earth belongs to us, but this is not the case. The lands and the seas belong to the beings of nature. We ourselves are only guests here because the elves and these invisible hidden nature spirits were here long before us humans. We should preserve this world, we

should heed the Earth-mother and nature and not destroy and poison them and exterminate other species.[5]

Erla's elves are nature spirits with a powerful ecological aspect to them. As such, they reflect the picture of elves and fairies that emerged from the sort of popular international culture that is dominated by the Anglophone world.

Erla's view of elves was also international in a further important respect. She refused to use only the categories of *álfar* (elves) and *huldufólk* (Hidden People) that had described the elves of Iceland's traditional narrative culture (see Chapter 1). Instead, she believed that the whole world was filled with a rich variety of different kinds of other-worldly beings. She argued that dwarves existed in lava and that there were fire spirits, moorland creatures, angels, light-elves and house dwarves that were said to enjoy clambering up and down bookshelves. Every tree, every flower and even every pot plant had its own fairy being. And so we find her writing in the introduction to her collection of stories:

> In our woodland areas there are all manner of woodland fairies and *ljúflingar* (darlings). There is a special being in every tree and flower. The woodland fairies are as beautiful to behold as young humans, many have wings, some look like big flies or butterflies. They correspond to the different types of trees.[6]

A little later she writes:

> If we have flowers, then there will also be flower elves in our homes. These are the most varied. During the summer months flower elves appear with multi-coloured wings.

There are also beings specific to the locale in every flower and pot plant. And you can see from them how the plant is faring.[7]

Since each individual plant has its own elf, Erla Stefánsdóttir's ideas about elves presuppose the existence of an incalculably large number of tiny creatures that are often winged and brightly coloured and that are inextricably linked to the growth of the flowers in question, the links being so close that Erla claims to be able to tell if her plants are healthy from the mere appearance of the elves that live on her pot plants. Despite this, there is no sense of overcrowding in this spiritual world of hers:

> The beings that I have enumerated cannot see one another as they are not all on the same wavelength or level.[8]

This ability of the different classes of elves and fairies to coexist on different wavelengths is one that Erla Stefánsdóttir compared to radio waves and to cordless telephones working alongside each other on different frequencies.

If Erla's elves, with their wings, their involvement in the growth of plants and their range of 'wavelengths', recall Edward L. Gardner's theosophical theories about the Cottingley fairies that we discussed in Chapter 6, then this should not come as a surprise because, like Gardner, Erla was a long-standing and committed member of the Theosophical Society, and in *Lífssýn mín* she describes in detail the influence of theosophical teachings on her thinking: as she herself used to emphasize, the tenets of theosophy were 'enlightening' for her. It is unsurprising, therefore, that her fairies were profoundly influenced by theosophical ideas, and that they have more in common with the theosophical interpretation of the Cottingley fairies than they do with the elves and fairies of traditional Icelandic folk culture. In the Icelandic folktales of the eighteenth and nineteenth centuries – and in evidence from rural parts of Iceland even as late as the twentieth century – concepts such as flower fairies, fairy wings and wavelengths are quite unknown. In comparison, Erla's urban fairies, which emerged under the influence of theosophy and popular international culture, are completely new phenomena that have little, or nothing, in common with the much older beliefs on the part of Iceland's rural population, whereas they correspond to international ideas about fairies from a much more recent period. Within the urban setting of the Reykjavík metropolitan region, elves and fairies have undergone a far-reaching transformative process that has altered them right down to their very essence.

The curious process by which Iceland's elves have been replaced by Reykjavík's fairies (at least in the area of the capital) can be observed in other ways, too. In 2006 and 2007, a group of social scientists in Iceland – Terry Gunnell, Ásdís Aðalbjörg Arnalds, Ragna Benedikta Garðarsdóttir and Unnur Diljá Teitsdóttir – undertook a large-scale study of the state of folk beliefs in contemporary Iceland. Several hundred Icelanders took part in the survey. Outside Iceland, this research remains famous above all for the question – one of many others – about the respondents' belief in elves. It was answered in 2006 by 602 participants in the survey. Some 15 per cent of those asked said that, for them, the existence of elves was inconceivable; 24 per cent thought their existence unlikely; 35 per cent thought it was possible; 18 per cent thought it probable; and 9 per cent regarded it as certain. This survey is regularly cited as evidence of a widespread belief in elves in the Icelandic population, since 85 per cent of those questioned refused to deny their existence outright. But what these figures might actually signify is by no means as clear as one might initially suppose. It is possible, after all, that some of those questioned claimed to believe in elves because a belief in elves had, in the meantime, become associated with the idea of Icelandic cultural identity. Substantially more interesting, therefore, are the other questions that were asked as part of this enquiry.

One of these questions was whether the participants in the survey drew a distinction between *álfar* (elves) and the *huldufólk* (Hidden People). In 2006, 647 respondents replied to this question. Of these, 54 per cent said no, 26 per cent admitted that they were not sure and 20 per cent said yes and agreed that they were able to tell the difference between elves and the Hidden People. This finding is interesting inasmuch as the two terms *álfar* and *huldufólk* were, for the most part, completely interchangeable in the folktales of the nineteenth century and were evidently used as synonyms. This finding shows that, for a relatively large number of people, this view has now changed. The differences between the various kinds of elves and fairies that Erla Stefánsdóttir was keen to distinguish have not yet been accepted by the majority of people, but have nonetheless been taken over by a broader cross-section of the population. In this way, the Icelanders' perception of elves and fairies has drawn closer to international images of them: here, too, different kinds of fairy exist alongside one another, just as Gardner postulated in his analysis of the Cottingley fairy photographs.

But it is in the answers to the question concerning Icelanders' views on the existence of 'flower elves' (*blómálfar*) that international influences are most clearly apparent. Of the 525 responses received in 2006, 25 per cent considered the existence of such elves inconceivable; 38 per cent thought that they were unlikely to exist; 26 per cent thought their existence a possibility; 7 per cent thought it likely; and 4 per cent believed that their existence was certain. What is interesting here is that, in the nineteenth century, 'flower elves' and 'flower fairies' were completely unknown in Iceland: the elves that featured in the traditional stories of the rural population were part of a hidden population that led parallel lives to the country's farmers. They had nothing to do with plants. Even the word *blómálfar* is relatively new, being a translation of the English 'flower fairies' that gave their name to the title of Cicely Mary Barker's successful series of children's books. Despite this, when participants in the survey were asked the ticklish question about flower fairies, the findings were not too far off those regarding the traditional terms used to describe elves: 4 per cent stated that they believed in flower fairies, while 9 per cent said that they believed in traditional Icelandic elves. Admittedly, there continues to be a distinction drawn between the two categories, inasmuch as a 'belief' in flower fairies is less pronounced than is claimed to be the case with traditional elves; but if we consider that flower fairies are newcomers to Iceland and, as such, are an invasive species, then they have made up for lost ground to a quite astonishing extent.

In Hafnarfjörður, the district of Reykjavík for which Erla Stefánsdóttir drew one of her famous 'elf maps' in 1993, there is now a café called Litla Álfabúðin, 'The Little Elf Shop'. There are guided tours to striking rock formations inhabited by the Hidden People within the precincts of the town, and in many of the small front gardens there are replicas of traditional turf houses inviting passers-by to dream of little elves. The Hellisgerði Municipal Park was, for a time, described on Google Maps as a 'Park with ponds, rocks & elves'. In Erla's eyes, this was one of the main places where elves could be found in the town. On her map of Hafnarfjörður, Hellisgerði showed the greatest concentration of supernatural beings within the town, elves, gnomes, Hidden People, dwarves and the 'Light of Belief' all being found here – and all of this in a park measuring barely 150 metres by 100 metres (3.7 acres) (Illus. 25).

Erla's map turned Hellisgerði into one of the most iconic elfin places of modern urban Iceland, certainly in the context of the way in which the island is marketed to tourists. Opened in 1922, the park is indeed an urban jewel, with its little winding pathways, gnarled trees, bizarre rock formations and tiny beds of brightly coloured flowers wherever there is sufficient protection from the harsh Icelandic winter for imported ornamental plants to grow. Hellisgerði is a fine example of Icelandic horticulture, demonstrating what can be achieved with the necessary care and when protected from the elements on this cold island in the North Atlantic. Nowhere else in Iceland does one have more of a feeling that Cicely Mary Barker's flower fairies might feel at home here. Her flower

25. Elf houses in Hellisgerði Municipal Park, Hafnarfjörður.

fairies would even be in tune with the ornamental statues in the park, whose pond is decorated with a bronze figure of a small child catching an outsize fish. Where children and flowers are as fixed a feature as they are in Hellisgerði, there flower fairies, too, can surely find a home.

But the irony is that nothing about Hellisgerði is 'natural'. Here in this park we can see what love and hard work may achieve even on a northern island like Iceland. In her writings Erla Stefánsdóttir stressed the connection between fairies and nature; but Hellisgerði is culture, not nature. The fact that her elves feel so much at home here in this urban and – albeit in a good way – artificial environment, where they are marketed at a Fairy Café and housed in cute little homes, is only one of many examples of the way in which her elfin mythology has its natural home in a city environment where international influences meet carefully manicured lawns and the artistic stylization of public green spaces. In a traditional rural environment Erla's elves would have been impossible. But the world is a changing place and through its parks and, in a more social context, through the local branch of the Theosophical Society, the metropolitan region of Reykjavík offered exactly the right setting for a comprehensive reinvention of Iceland's elves, allowing them to meet a new international standard.

A Glance Backwards and into the Future

CHAPTER 8

COMING FULL CIRCLE AND THE TAMING OF THE FAIRIES

With the fairies of Iceland's 'Elves' Representative' our journey has brought us back to its point of origin – or at least to somewhere close to that point. The great cultural and historical trajectory that this study has pursued began in rural Iceland, whose elves, residing in their elf hills, were the closest neighbours of the inhabitants of many ancient farmsteads, and where these *álfar* formed a 'hidden' society that flourished in parallel with the rural communities of the period, adding a little more life to a landscape that was all too barren. Many of the motifs from traditional Icelandic popular belief and from the world of Icelandic folktales found a counterpart in Ireland, whose world of myths and legends left a lasting mark on that of Iceland, for all that it revealed a somewhat different character. Iceland's Hidden People generally lived alongside the human population and proved to be good neighbours, only rarely taking revenge for human encroachments on their world (even if those acts of retribution could sometimes assume the most drastic forms), while two qualities above all stood out in Ireland: in its medieval literature it was the glamour that was stressed, whereas later folktales focused more on the darker aspects of fairies. In the Ireland of the modern period, the death of children and of young people in the first flush of life was explained by reference to the tales of changelings, so that the underlying tone of the world of legends grew noticeably darker than it ever had been in Iceland.

From Ireland we followed the cultural history of elves and fairies to the courtly literature of the High Middle Ages, which played in particular with motifs that had already been repeatedly treated centuries earlier in Irish literature. Here we met powerful female fairies who lived on the Isle of Avalon in Arthurian literature and in the fairy forests of the Breton *lais*, and whose literary treatment continued to reverberate in the descriptions of fairies in traditional Scottish ballads. Perhaps the two most famous ballads were the ones about Thomas the Rhymer and Tam Lin, and it is here in particular that we can still hear clear echoes of the older courtly poems. Leaving the courtly world, we traced the development of elves and fairies as they made their way into towns and cities in the sixteenth and seventeenth centuries. While Scottish witch trials persecuted people for their alleged or self-confessed dealings with the fairy world, and while James VI of Scotland, writing in his *Daemonologie*, equated the world of fairies with that of Satan, Shakespeare was bringing elves and fairies to the urban theatre, in *A Midsummer Night's Dream* and in *Romeo and Juliet*. The simultaneous persecution of witches in the real world and the representation of elves and fairies on stage is not only tragic in terms of the fate of the victims of these witch trials, it is also iconic when we examine the developments of the age, when attempts were made to drive fairies from their Scottish rural habitat, while welcoming them into the world of the urban theatre in England.

The late eighteenth and early nineteenth centuries witnessed not only the emergence of the modern picture of the fairy as a tiny anthropomorphic creature with an insect's wings, but also the arrival of elves and fairies on the arts scene in towns and cities up and down the country. Both of these developments can be traced back to a circle of artists that was active in London in the years around 1800 and that included William Blake and Henry Fuseli. They culminated in the Victorian fairy paintings that celebrated the portrayal of elves and fairies in the visual arts in ways never equalled either before or since. With the establishment of folklore as a subject for scholarly enquiry through the efforts of Jacob and Wilhelm Grimm, the nineteenth century also witnessed the first systematic examination of the narrative traditions of the 'common people', an examination undertaken for the edification of a well-to-do urban bourgeoisie. The wealth of material that became available to these privileged circles led to a proliferation of fairy motifs not only in art but in literature, too.

But this rise in the fairies' popularity went hand in hand with a decline in their fortunes; for although they may have become the darlings of a middle-class audience, they also grew increasingly shrivelled in size. The traditional fairies of Iceland and Ireland had been the size of humans, whom they also resembled, but in a bourgeois setting they were turned more and more into tiny creatures with insect wings. By the early twentieth century, this type of fairy had achieved extraordinary success in the Tinker Bell of Barrie's *Peter Pan* and in the Cottingley fairy photographs. This was now the only way in which fairies could be imagined. But this also meant that they were largely stripped of their powers – a process that, at its worst, reduced these once dangerous, inscrutable creatures of the otherworld to the personification of photosynthesis and cell growth. Rarely, if ever, have fairies been as robbed of their power and initiative as was the case with the theosophical interpretations of the Cottingley fairies. The female rulers of Avalon, from whose magic no knight could escape and who even received King Arthur into their midst at the very end of his life, had become tiny, semiconscious creatures with the intelligence of puppies, their sole purpose in life now being to ensure that flowers were the right colour.

But a countermovement soon developed, determined to resist this reductive process. It was a development influenced in no small part by J.R.R. Tolkien, whose programmatical use of medieval fairy stories left a lasting mark on the genre of fantasy fiction that evolved in the wake of the Second World War. And yet the rise of the 'flower fairy' in the early twentieth century was by now completely unstoppable, and ever since then tiny, insect-like fairies have been a prominent part of modern ideas about fairies and of the way in which the fairy world is depicted in art. This is also true of the field of alternative religions and spiritualities, where these fairies are to be found again and again in the records of the Fairy Investigation Society, and retained their prominence in writings influenced by the theosophical movement. At the same time, however, these fairies achieved a new and greater relevance in the wake of wider developments that have seen them as 'nature spirits' particularly keen to protect nature in the face of the present-day despoliation and pollution of the environment.

The rise of the 'eco-fairy' as an important figure in our picture of fairies in recent decades finally brought us back to Iceland, where every few years fairies make the international headlines by becoming figureheads in the movement to protect the natural countryside from modern infrastructure projects. 'Elf lobby stops building project', ran a headline in the prominent German newspaper *Süddeutsche Zeitung* on 23 December 2013, while the same incident was described in the Swiss *Neue Zürcher Zeitung* three days later under the heading 'A country takes heed of elves'. The fascination with which these and similar events are followed in the international press is evidence of the widespread desire to invest our world with a new sense of magic and wonderment. At the same time, reports about Icelandic seers and mediums who refer to creatures from the world of elves when having their say on questions relating to the environment are likewise rooted in real life. Erla Stefánsdóttir, who became known in the German-speaking world as the 'Elves' Representative in Iceland', repeatedly expressed her views on the environment and saw the protection of the world around us as a spiritual obligation. In her writings, the elves of the North Atlantic island are routinely compared to the flower fairies of international popular culture and aligned with the theoretical constructs of theosophy, as promulgated by Edward L. Gardner in his contributions to the debate about the photographs of the Cottingley fairies, which he interpreted from his own theosophical standpoint. And so we come (almost) full circle: just as was the case in the early Middle Ages, the images of fairies from the British Isles – in other words, from international Anglophone popular culture – have reached Iceland, where they have been instrumental in refashioning the island's view of elves and fairies. The way in which these influences have been comprehensively reworked and turned into a new theory about Icelandic elves in the writings of a theosophist like Erla Stefánsdóttir is only another instance of this development; but it is basically the same phenomenon as can now be seen in the omnipresence of flower fairies in public spaces in Iceland, whether it be on the shelves of souvenir shops or in the surprising frequency with which Icelanders assert their belief in flower fairies, or *blómálfar*.

In tracing a line of development from the elves of traditional rural Iceland to the flower fairies of Reykjavík I have tried to demonstrate how we have reached a point where completely different ideas about elves now stand side by side in Iceland. In Iceland – as in other parts of Europe – different concepts coexist. They all emerged in multiple contexts over the course of a long historical development, before being taken up in other regions as a result of the close links that have always characterized the history of European religions and cultures. The question of how these different types of elf can exist alongside each other in Iceland has also provided us with an opportunity to sketch out a basic outline of the cultural history of elves and fairies: European history is such a tight-knit network that even the cultural history of relatively small areas can be understood only from a broader European perspective.

Although – or precisely because – my aim has been to summarize the basic outlines and essential developments in attitudes to elves and fairies in European cultural and religious history, it has been possible to present only a small selection of the vast wealth of European fairy traditions and the artistic and literary products that have resulted from this development. It was simply not possible to find the space to discuss even such literary masterpieces from recent decades as Susanna Clarke's *Jonathan Strange & Mr Norrell* (2004) and Sylvia Townsend Warner's *Kingdoms of Elfin* (1977). The same is true of the elves and fairies that have found new homes in the cinema, in computer games and in role-playing. By the same token, the reception of elves and fairies in contemporary trends in the various alternative religions is multifaceted in ways that I have barely been able to hint at. Historical theories on the origins of stories about elves influenced Gerald B. Gardner when writing *Witchcraft Today* (1954), one of the foundational texts of the Wicca movement; and this in turn found a literary reflex in Marion Zimmer Bradley's international bestseller *The Mists of Avalon* (1983). Even entire motivic complexes have not been discussed, including that of the Good Fairy who grants the wishes of people who need her help and who are worthy of it. Today's audiences are familiar with the figure of the Good Fairy more especially from *Cinderella* in the form first found in the fairytale from 1697 by the French writer of such tales, Charles Perrault, and later in the film version by Walt Disney (1950). Nor has there been any room for the whole of the Italian fairy tradition, starting with the term Fata Morgana (literally, the 'Fairy Morgana') that was used to describe the optical illusions seen on the Strait of Messina, and culminating in Carlo Collodi's *Pinocchio* of 1883, in which the Blue-Haired Fairy rescues Pinocchio and ultimately turns him into a proper boy. Not even the rich traditions from Wales could be included here: among these are the otherworld narratives of the medieval *Mabinogion* and the modern accounts of the *Tylwyth Teg*.

But the majority of these tales of elves and fairies could have been inserted at the appropriate points in the foregoing sketch in the earlier chapters. In recent decades the increasing appropriation of elves and fairies by the urban population has led to changes similar to the ones already outlined, one of which is the loss of a specifically local element. In Ireland, tales about changelings are a significant part of the folk tradition, whereas they have been rarely found in Iceland. Brownies are a particular feature of popular legend in Scotland and Northern England, but in Ireland they are found only in families with close links with Great Britain. The traditional mythology of elves and fairies is specific to individual regions and by no means the same in every country. But in their reception in fairy romances of recent decades, these differences have generally been obscured and replaced by the suggestion of a uniform otherworld. The local element has been lost even more strikingly in the way in which traditional tales about elves and fairies were tied to a particular place: in rural Iceland and Ireland the fairies lived in a specific rock or a specific mound. In modern urban retellings, elves and fairies have broken free from these very particular locations and now belong to a delocalized fairy world that is tied to no particular place. Even in those instances where they are still linked to the land, they are no longer bound to a particular rock formation but only to a generalized concept of 'nature'.

A further change that has kept recurring is the marked reduction in the size of elves and fairies – and not just in terms of their physical dimensions. Even the fairies whom Shakespeare introduced to the urban stages of the Tudor period could hide in an acorn, in that way anticipating the urban elves of the metropolitan region of Reykjavík, where, according to Erla Stefánsdóttir, every pot plant has its own elf. The elves that, in their differing ways, held sway over the land and the countryside in traditional rural areas were stripped of their power when relocated to urban contexts, resulting in a reduction in their stature. The elf who could wipe out an entire family to punish them for destroying a meadow is reduced to the level of a harmless flower fairy. And so the fairies who were moved to an urban environment were not only shrunk, they were also tamed. Even in those instances where the forces of the otherworld are treated as real by the proponents of alternative spiritualities, elves and fairies no longer enjoy the status of their historical predecessors. Far from fearing them, people nowadays hope to meet them — an encounter that every peasant woman and every fisherman in Gaelic Ireland once sought to avoid at all costs.

In general, we can best describe the contrast between urban elves and fairies and their traditional rural counterparts by saying that every age and every stratum in society has its own otherworld that reflects its fears, its longings and its needs. The traditional elves of Icelandic folktales were an answer to the oppressive emptiness of the country, while the nature spirits of modern towns and cities are a response to the longings felt by people who have been alienated from the land and who yearn for a return to nature. On one level, elves and fairies are a means by which to articulate longings that might otherwise remain only half-conscious. As such, they indicate what it is that motivates a particular society. Against this background, this trend to tame and diminish elves and fairies that we can observe at a time of growing concern for the environment is remarkable, to say the least. As modern 'eco-fairies' they are astonishingly lacking in any sense of menace. What does our yearning for such a tamed world of fairies say about our present age?

ENDNOTES

Introduction
1. Jacob and Wilhelm Grimm (eds), *Deutsches Wörterbuch*, 33 vols, Verlag S. Hirzel, Leipzig, 1854–1984, iii.400.
2. Diane Purkiss, *Fairies and Fairy Stories: A History*, Tempus, Stroud, 2007, 7.

Chapter 1
1. Snorri Sturluson, *Edda*, trans. Anthony Faulkes, J.M. Dent, London, 1995, 19–20 (in the original, *Gylfaginning*, ch. 17).
2. Stefán Pálsson, 'Þiðriksvellir (Strandasýsla, Hrófbergshreppur)'. Unpublished typescript in the archive of Stofnun Árna Magnússonar í íslenskum fræðum in Reykjavík, available at https://nafnid.is/ornefnaskra/17624.

Chapter 2
1. Vernam Hull, 'De Gabáil in t-Šída (Concerning the Seizure of the Fairy Mound)', *Zeitschrift für celtische Philologie*, xix (1933), 53–8, esp. 56.
2. Adapted after Tom P. Cross and Clark Harris Slover (eds), *Ancient Irish Tales*, Barnes & Noble, New York, 1996, 488.

Chapter 3
1. Diane Purkiss, *Fairies and Fairy Stories: A History*, Tempus, Stroud, 2007, 77–8.

Chapter 4

1. William Shakespeare, *The Complete Plays: Tragicomedies*, ed. Stanley Wells and Gary Taylor, The Folio Society, London, 1997, 24.
2. King James the First, *Daemonologie (1597). Newes from Scotland (1591)*, ed. G.B. Harrison, John Lane, London and E.P. Dutton, New York, 1924, 73–4.

Chapter 5

1. Alexander Pope, *The Rape of the Lock: An Heroi-Comical Poem in Five Canto's*, The Folio Press, London, 1989, 18–19.
2. John Adlard, 'Mr. Blake's fairies', *Neuphilologische Mitteilungen*, lxv (1964), 144–60, esp. 144.
3. Walter Scott, *Minstrelsy of the Scottish Border*, 2 vols, T. Cadell and W. Davies, London, 1802, ii.187.
4. W.B. Yeats, *Poems*, T. Fisher Unwin, London, 1901, 214.
5. D.E.D.I. (W.B. Yeats), 'Invoking the Irish fairies', *The Irish Theosophist*, i (1892), 6.
6. Lady Gregory, *Gods and Fighting Men*, with a preface by W.B. Yeats and a foreword by Daniel J. Murphy, Colin Smythe Limited, Gerrards Cross, 2006, 16.

Chapter 6

1. J.M. Barrie, *Peter Pan or The Boy Who Would Not Grow Up*, Hodder and Stoughton, London, 1928, 33–4.
2. Ibid., 28–9.
3. Ibid., 32.
4. Arthur Conan Doyle, *The Coming of the Fairies*, Hodder and Stoughton, London, 1922, 41.
5. Ibid., 122.
6. Ibid., 123.
7. Ibid., 124.
8. Simon Young, 'A history of the Fairy Investigation Society, 1927–1960', *Folklore*, cxxiv (2013), 139–56, esp. 141.
9. Bernard Sleigh, *The Gates of Horn*, Aldine House, London, 1926, ix.
10. Simon Young, 'Introduction', in Marjorie T. Johnson, *Seeing Fairies: From the Lost Archives of the Fairy Investigation Society, Authentic Reports of Fairies in Modern Times*, Anomalist Books, San Antonio, TX, 2014, vii–xxiv, esp. ix and xix.
11. Johnson, *Seeing Fairies* (note 10), 51.
12. Ibid., 71–2.
13. Ibid., 72.

Chapter 7

1. J.R.R. Tolkien, *On Fairy-stories*, ed. Verlyn Flieger and Douglas A. Anderson, HarperCollins, London, 2008, 29–30.
2. Andrew Lang (ed.), *The Lilac Fairy Book*, Longmans, Green, and Co., London, 1910, viii.
3. J.R.R. Tolkien, *The Two Towers*, HarperCollins, London, 2011, 48.
4. Eoin Colfer, *Artemis Fowl*, Viking, London, 2001, 68.
5. Erla Stefánsdóttir, *Erlas Elfengeschichten: Die 'isländische Elfenbeauftragte' erzählt*, trans. Hiltrud Hildur Guðmundsdóttir, Verlag Neue Erde, Saarbrücken, 2011, 10.
6. Ibid., 12.
7. Ibid., 13.
8. Ibid.

FURTHER READING

The following titles do not constitute a complete bibliography on the subject of elves and fairies, but list only the most important sources used in the respective chapters, at least to the extent that these sources cannot be identified within the chapters themselves, and recommend a small selection of texts as starting points for further reading. In keeping with Icelandic conventions, Icelandic writers are listed alphabetically according to their *first* names.

Introduction

Sources

Grimm, Jacob and Wilhelm (eds). *Deutsches Wörterbuch*, 33 vols, Verlag S. Hirzel, Leipzig, 1854–1984

Purkiss, Diane. *Fairies and Fairy Stories: A History*, Tempus, Stroud, 2007

Shippey, Tom. '*Alias oves habeo*: The elves as a category problem', in Tom Shippey (ed.), *The Shadow-Walkers: Jacob Grimm's Mythology of the Monstrous*, Arizona Centre for Medieval and Renaissance Studies, Tempe, AZ, 2005, 157–87

Further Reading: General Titles on Elves and Fairies

Briggs, Katharine. *An Encyclopedia of Fairies, Hobgoblins, Brownies, Bogies, and Other Supernatural Creatures*, Pantheon, New York, 1978 (published by Penguin in 1976 as *A Dictionary of Fairies, Hobgoblins, Brownies, Bogies, and Other Supernatural Creatures*)

Harte, Jeremy. *Explore Fairy Traditions*, 2nd edn, Heart of Albion Press, Orson, 2022 (open access: https://www.hoap.co.uk/explore_fairy_traditions.pdf)

Narváez, Peter (ed.). *The Good People: New Fairylore Essays*, Garland, New York, 1991

Ostling, Michael (ed.). *Fairies, Demons, and Nature Spirits: 'Small Gods' at the Margins of Christendom*, Palgrave Macmillan, London, 2018

Purkiss, Diane. *Fairies and Fairy Stories: A History*, Tempus, Stroud, 2007

Young, Simon and Davide Ermacora (eds). *The Exeter Companion to Fairies, Nereids, Trolls and Other Social Supernatural Beings: European Traditions*, University of Exeter Press, Exeter, 2024

Young, Simon and Ceri Houlbrook (eds). *Magical Folk: British and Irish Fairies, 500 AD to the Present*, Gibson Square Books, London, 2018

Chapter 1

Sources

Ármann Jakobsson. 'Beware of the elf! A note on the evolving meaning of *álfar*', *Folklore*, cxxvi (2015), 215–23

Egeler, Matthias. 'Iceland: The elves of Strandir', in Simon Young and Davide Ermacora (eds), *The Exeter Companion to Fairies, Nereids, Trolls and Other Social Supernatural Beings: European Traditions*, University of Exeter Press, Exeter, 2024, 71–86

Einar Ólafur Sveinsson. *The Folk-Stories of Iceland*, Viking Society for Northern Research, London, 2003

Gunnell, Terry. 'How Elvish were the *álfar*?', in Andrew Wawn and others (eds), *Constructing Nations, Reconstructing Myth*, Brepols, Turnhout, 2007, 111–30

——. 'Álfar (Elves)', in Jens Peter Schjødt and others (eds), *The Pre-Christian Religions of the North: Histories and Structures*, 4 vols, Brepols, Turnhout, 2020, iii.1571–80

Hall, Alaric. *Elves in Anglo-Saxon England: Matters of Belief, Health, Gender and Identity*, Boydell & Brewer, Woodbridge, 2007

Maurer, Konrad. *Isländische Volkssagen der Gegenwart*, J.C. Hinrichs, Leipzig, 1860

Further Reading

Almqvist, Bo. '*Midwife to the fairies* (ML 5070) in Icelandic tradition' and '*Midwife to the fairies* in Iceland: A variant list', in Terry Gunnell (ed.), *Legends and Landscape: Plenary Papers from the 5th Celtic-Nordic-Baltic Folklore Symposium, Reykjavík 2005*, University of Iceland Press, Reykjavík, 2008, 273–342

Ármann Jakobsson. 'The extreme emotional life of Völundr the elf', *Scandinavian Studies*, lxxviii (2006), 227–54

Egeler, Matthias. *Landscape, Religion, and the Supernatural: Nordic Perspectives on Landscape Theory*, Oxford University Press, New York, 2024 (open access: https://doi.org/10.1093/oso/9780197747360.001.0001)
Egeler, Matthias, Dagrún Ósk Jónsdóttir and Jón Jónsson. 'Patterns in Icelandic Elf Hills', *Folklore*, cxxxv (2024), 388–414 (open access: https://doi.org/10.1080/0015587X.2024.2359778)
Egeler, Matthias and Jón Jónsson (eds and transl.). *The Treatise on Elves by Ólafur of Purkey: Cosmology and Folk Belief in Nineteenth-Century Iceland*. Helsinki, Kalevala Society Foundation, forthcoming.
Einar Ólafur Sveinsson. *The Folk-Stories of Iceland*, Viking Society for Northern Research, London, 2003
Gunnell, Terry. 'The *álfar*, the clerics and the Enlightenment: Conceptions of the supernatural in the Age of Reason in Iceland', in Michael Ostling (ed.), *Fairies, Demons, and Nature Spirits: 'Small Gods' at the Margins of Christendom*, Palgrave Macmillan, London, 2018, 191–212
Schjødt, Jens Peter, John Lindow and Anders Andrén (eds). *The Pre-Christian Religions of the North: Histories and Structures*, 4 vols, Brepols, Turnhout, 2020
Simek, Rudolf. 'Elves and exorcism: Runic and other lead amulets in medieval popular religion', in Daniel Anlezark (ed.), *Myths, Legends and Heroes: Essays on Old Norse and Old English Literature in Honour of John McKinnell*, University of Toronto Press, Toronto/Buffalo/London, 2011, 25–52
——. 'On elves', in Stefan Brink and Lisa Collinson (eds), *Theorizing Old Norse Myth*, Brepols, Turnhout, 2017, 195–223

Chapter 2

Sources

Bourke, Angela. *The Burning of Bridget Cleary: A True Story*, 2nd edn, Penguin, London, 2006
Carey, John. *The Mythological Cycle of Medieval Irish Literature*, Cork Studies in Celtic Literature, Cork, 2018
Egeler, Matthias. *Vom Land der Frauen und keltischen Helden: Irische Erzählungen von den Inseln der Unsterblichkeit*, Praesens, Vienna, 2016
Lady Gregory. *Visions and Beliefs in the West of Ireland, Collected and Arranged by Lady Gregory; With Two Essays and Notes by W.B. Yeats*, 2 vols, G.P. Putnam's Sons, New York, 1920
Jones, Bryan J. and W.B. Yeats. 'Traditions and superstitions collected at Kilcurry, County Louth, Ireland', *Folklore*, x (1899), 119–23
Narváez, Peter (ed.). *The Good People: New Fairylore Essays*, Garland, New York, 1991
Ó hEochaidh, Seán (collector), Máire Mac Néill (translator) and Séamas Ó Catháin (editor of Irish texts). *Síscéalta ó Thír Chonaill: Fairy Legends from Donegal*, Folklore Department of the University of Dublin, Dublin, 1977
Young, Simon and Ceri Houlbrook (eds). *Magical Folk: British and Irish Fairies, 500 AD to the Present*, Gibson Square Books, London, 2018

Further Reading

Carey, John. *A Single Ray of the Sun: Religious Speculation in Early Ireland*, Celtic Studies Publications, Andover/Aberystwyth, 1999
Evans Wentz, W.Y. *The Fairy-Faith in Celtic Countries*, Henry Frowde, London, 1911
Hyde, Douglas (ed.). *Sgéalta Thomáis Uí Chathasaigh: Mayo Stories, Told by Thomas Casey*, Irish Texts Society, London, 1939
MacManus, Dermot A. *The Middle Kingdom: The Faerie World of Ireland*, Colin Smythe, Gerrards Cross, 1973
Thurneysen, Rudolf. *Die irische Helden- und Königsage bis zum siebzehnten Jahrhundert*, Niemeyer, Halle (Saale), 1921
Williams, Mark. *Ireland's Immortals: A History of the Gods of Irish Myth*, Princeton University Press, Princeton, NJ, 2016
——. *The Celtic Myths That Shape the Way We Think*, Thames & Hudson, London/New York, 2021
Young, Simon. 'Fairy impostors in County Longford in the Great Famine', *Studia Hibernica*, xxxviii (2012), 181–99

A wealth of studies of Irish fairy traditions have been published in *Béaloideas*, the journal of the Folklore of Ireland Society.

Chapter 3

Sources

Barrett, W.P. *The Trial of Jeanne d'Arc*, Gotham House, New York, 1932
Burgess, Glyn S. and Leslie C. Brook (ed. and transl. with the collaboration of Amanda Hopkins). *French Arthurian Literature IV: Eleven Old French Narrative Lays*, D.S. Brewer, Woodbridge/Rochester, 2007
Burgess, Glyn S. and Keith Busby. *The Lais of Marie de France*, Penguin, London, 1999
Child, Francis James (ed.). *The English and Scottish Popular Ballads*, 5 vols, Houghton, Mifflin and Company, Boston, 1882–98
Clarke, Basil. *Life of Merlin. Geoffrey of Monmouth: Vita Merlini*, University of Wales Press, Cardiff, 1973
Egeler, Matthias. *Avalon, 66° Nord*, De Gruyter, Berlin, 2015
Knapp, Fritz Peter. *Altfranzösische Erzählungen von keltischen Feen*, Praesens, Vienna, 2016
Simek, Rudolf. *Artus-Lexikon*, Reclam, Stuttgart, 2012

Further Reading

Clark, John. *The Green Children of Woolpit: Chronicles, Fairies and Facts in Medieval England*, Exeter University Press, Exeter, 2024
Flood, Victoria. *Fantastic Histories: Medieval Fairy Narratives and the Limits of Wonder*, Manchester University Press, Manchester, 2024
Green, Richard Firth. *Elf Queens and Holy Friars: Fairy Beliefs and the Medieval Church*, University of Pennsylvania Press, Philadelphia, 2016

Harte, Jeremy. *Fairy Encounters in Medieval England: Landscape, Folklore and the Supernatural*, University of Exeter Press, Exeter, 2024

Larrington, Carolyne. *King Arthur's Enchantresses: Morgan and Her Sisters in Arthurian Tradition*, I.B. Tauris, London/New York, 2006

Maraschi, Andrea. 'The Tree of the Bourlémonts. Gendered beliefs in fairies and their transmission from old to young women in Joan of Arc's Domrémy', in Marina Montesano (ed.), *Folklore, Magic, and Witchcraft: Cultural Exchanges from the Twelfth to Eighteenth Century*, Routledge, London, 2021, 21–32

Paton, Lucy Allen. *Studies in the Fairy Mythology of Arthurian Romance*, 2nd edn, Franklin, New York, 1960

Young, Francis. *Twilight of the Godlings: The Shadowy Beginnings of Britain's Supernatural Beings.* Cambridge University Press, Cambridge, 2023

Chapter 4

Sources

Hall, Alaric. 'Folk-healing, fairies and witchcraft: The trial of Stein Maltman, Stirling 1628', *Studia Celtica Fennica*, iii (2006), 10–25

Henderson, Lizanne and Edward J. Cowan. *Scottish Fairy Belief: A History*, John Donald, East Linton, 2001

Hutton, Ronald. 'The making of the early modern British fairy tradition', *Historical Journal*, lvii (2014), 1135–56

Kirk, Robert. *The Secret Common-Wealth & A Short Treatise of Charms and Spells*, ed. Stewart Sanderson, D.S. Brewer, London, 1976

——. *The Secret Commonwealth of Elves, Fauns, and Fairies*, Introduction by Marina Warner, New York Review of Books, New York, 2007 (modernized orthography)

Pitcairn, Robert. *Ancient Criminal Trials in Scotland*, Vol. III, Part 2, Bannatyne Club, Edinburgh, 1833 (documents relating to the trial of Isobel Gowdie appear here on pp. 602–16)

Further Reading

Buccola, Regina. *Fairies, Fractious Women, and the Old Faith: Fairy Lore in Early Modern British Drama and Culture*, Susquehanna University Press, Selinsgrove, PA, 2006

Henderson, Lizanne and Edward J. Cowan. *Scottish Fairy Belief: A History*, John Donald, East Linton, 2001

Lamb, Mary Ellen. *The Popular Culture of Shakespeare, Spenser and Jonson*, Routledge, Milton Park/New York, 2006

Latham, Minor White. *The Elizabethan Fairies: The Fairies of Folklore and the Fairies of Shakespeare*, Columbia University Press, New York, 1930

Purkiss, Diane. *Fairies and Fairy Stories: A History*, Tempus, Stroud, 2007

Wilby, Emma. *The Visions of Isobel Gowdie: Magic, Witchcraft and Dark Shamanism in Seventeenth-Century Scotland*, Liverpool University Press, Eastbourne, 2010

Chapter 5

Sources

Adlard, John. 'Mr. Blake's fairies', *Neuphilologische Mitteilungen*, lxv (1964), 144–60

Berner, Hannah. '"Her Oluf hand rider saa vide": Stationen der Wanderung einer dänischen Ballade von Herder bis Heine', in Franz Zipfel (ed.), *Fremde Ähnlichkeiten: Die 'Große Wanderung' als Herausforderung der Komparatistik*, J.B. Metzler, Stuttgart, 2017, 114–39

Böldl, Klaus and Katarina Yngborn. *Ritter und Elfen, Liebe und Tod: Nordische Balladen des Mittelalters*, C.H. Beck, Munich, 2011

Bown, Nicola. *Fairies in Nineteenth-Century Art and Literature*, Cambridge University Press, Cambridge, 2001

Martineau, Jane (ed.). *Victorian Fairy Painting*, Merrell Holberton/Royal Academy of Arts, London, 1997

Pfeifer, Wolfgang and others. *Etymologisches Wörterbuch des Deutschen*, Akademie Verlag, Berlin, 1993

Silver, Carole G. *Strange and Secret Peoples: Fairies and Victorian Consciousness*, Oxford University Press, Oxford, 1999

Williams, Mark. *Ireland's Immortals: A History of the Gods of Irish Myth*, Princeton University Press, Princeton, NJ, 2016

Wood, Christopher. *Fairies in Victorian Art*, 2nd edn, Antique Collectors' Club, Woodbridge, 2008

Young, Simon. 'Fairies and railways: A nineteenth-century topos and its origins', *Notes and Queries*, lix/3 (2012), 401–3

——. 'When did fairies get wings?', in Darryl Caterine and John W. Morehead (eds), *The Paranormal and Popular Culture: A Postmodern Religious Landscape*, Routledge, London, 2020, 253–74

Further Reading

Bown, Nicola. *Fairies in Nineteenth-Century Art and Literature*, Cambridge University Press, Cambridge, 2001

Gunnell, Terry (ed.). *Grimm Ripples: The Legacy of the Grimms' Deutsche Sagen in Northern Europe*, Brill, Leiden/Boston, 2022

Martineau, Jane (ed.). *Victorian Fairy Painting*, Merrell Holberton/Royal Academy of Arts, London, 1997

Shippey, Tom (ed.). *The Shadow-Walkers: Jacob Grimm's Mythology of the Monstrous*, Arizona Center for Medieval and Renaissance Studies, Tempe, 2005

Silver, Carole G. *Strange and Secret Peoples: Fairies and Victorian Consciousness*, Oxford University Press, Oxford, 1999

Smith, Peter Alderson. *W.B. Yeats and the Tribes of Danu: Three Views of Ireland's Fairies*, Colin Smythe, Gerrards Cross, 1986

Taylor, Lynda. 'The Cultural Significance of Elves in Northern European Balladry', PhD thesis, University of Leeds, 2014 (open access: https://etheses.whiterose.ac.uk/id/eprint/8759/)

Williams, Mark. *Ireland's Immortals: A History of the Gods of Irish Myth*, Princeton University Press, Princeton, NJ, 2016

Wood, Christopher. *Fairies in Victorian Art*, 2nd edn, Antique Collectors' Club, Woodbridge, 2008

A wealth of studies of international folkloric fairy traditions (not only) since the nineteenth century has been published in *Folklore*, the journal of the Folklore Society, based in London.

Chapter 6

Sources

Barrie, J.M. *Peter Pan in Kensington Gardens* and *Peter and Wendy*, ed. Peter Hollindale, Oxford University Press, Oxford, 1991

Cooper, Roger. 'Bernard Sleigh, artist and craftsman, 1872–1954', *The Journal of the Decorative Arts Society*, xxi (1997), 88–102

Cottingley Fairies Collection. Archives of the University of Leeds, available online at https://explore.library.leeds.ac.uk/special-collections-explore/8705

Doyle, Arthur Conan. *The Coming of the Fairies*, Hodder and Stoughton, Toronto/London/New York, 1922

Johnson, Marjorie T. *Seeing Fairies: From the Lost Archives of the Fairy Investigation Society. Authentic Reports of Fairies in Modern Times*, Anomalist Books, San Antonio, TX, 2014

Purkiss, Diane. *Fairies and Fairy Stories: A History*, Tempus, Stroud, 2007

Smith, Paul. 'The Cottingley fairies: The end of a legend', in Peter Narváez (ed.), *The Good People: New Fairylore Essays*, Garland, New York, 1991, 371–405

Young, Simon. 'A history of the Fairy Investigation Society, 1927–1960', *Folklore*, cxxiv (2013), 139–56

——. 'Introduction', in Marjorie T. Johnson, *Seeing Fairies: From the Lost Archives of the Fairy Investigation Society. Authentic Reports of Fairies in Modern Times*, Anomalist Books, San Antonio, TX, 2014, vii–xxiv

Further Reading

Bergman, Jenni. 'The Significant Other: A Literary History of Elves', PhD thesis, Cardiff University, 2011 (open access: https://orca.cardiff.ac.uk/id/eprint/55478/)

Cooper, Joe. *The Case of the Cottingley Fairies*, Robert Hale, London, 1990

Young, Simon (ed.). *The Cottingley Fairy Photographs: New Approaches to Fairies, Fakes and Folklore*, Pwca Books and Pamphlets, no place, 2024

Chapter 7

Sources

Briggs, Katharine. *An Encyclopedia of Fairies, Hobgoblins, Brownies, Bogies, and Other Supernatural Creatures*, Pantheon, New York, 1978

(published by Penguin in 1976 as *A Dictionary of Fairies, Hobgoblins, Brownies, Bogies, and Other Supernatural Creatures*)

Erla Stefánsdóttir. *Lífssýn mín: Lebenseinsichten der isländischen Elfenbeauftragten*, trans. Hiltrud Hildur Guðmundsdóttir, Verlag Neue Erde, Saarbrücken, 2007

——. *Erlas Elfengeschichten: Die 'isländische Elfenbeauftragte' erzählt*, trans. Hiltrud Hildur Guðmundsdóttir, Verlag Neue Erde, Saarbrücken, 2011

Letcher, Andy. 'The scouring of the shire: Fairies, trolls and pixies in eco-protest culture', *Folklore*, cxii (2001), 147–61

Magliocco, Sabina. 'Reconnecting to everything: Fairies in contemporary paganism', in Michael Ostling (ed.), *Fairies, Demons, and Nature Spirits: 'Small Gods' at the Margins of Christendom*, Palgrave Macmillan, London, 2018, 325–47

——. 'The taming of the fae: Literary and folkloric fairies in modern paganisms', in Shai Feraro and Ethan Doyle White (eds), *Magic and Witchery in the Modern West: Celebrating the Twentieth Anniversary of 'The Triumph of the Moon'*, Palgrave Macmillan, London, 2019, 107–30

Further Reading

Bergman, Jenni. 'The Significant Other: A Literary History of Elves', PhD thesis, Cardiff University, 2011 (open access: https://orca.cardiff.ac.uk/id/eprint/55478/)

Letcher, Andy. ' "There's bulldozers in the fairy garden": Re-enchantment narratives within British eco-paganism', in Lynne Hume and Kathleen McPhillips (eds), *Popular Spiritualities: The Politics of Contemporary Enchantment*, Ashgate, Aldershot/Burlington, VT, 2006, 175–86

Shippey, Tom. 'Light-elves, dark-elves, and others: Tolkien's elvish problem', *Tolkien Studies*, i (2004), 1–15

Tracy, Tony. 'When Disney met Delargy: "Darby O'Gill" and the Irish Folklore Commission', *Béaloideas*, lxxviii (2010), 44–60

Valdimar Tr. Hafstein. 'The elves' point of view: Cultural identity in contemporary Icelandic elf-tradition', *Fabula: Zeitschrift für Erzählforschung*, xli (2000), 87–104

Young, Simon. 'Walt and the Fairies: 1922–1960', in Joshua Cutchin (ed.), *Fairy Films: Wee Folk on the Big Screen*, Educated Dragon, no place, 2023, 213–29

—— (ed.). *Fairy Census, 2014–2017*, 1st edn, 8 January 2018 (open access: https://www.academia.edu/35591008/The_Fairy_Census_2014_2017_pdf)

—— (ed.). *Fairy Census 2 (2017–2023)*, 2nd edn, 12 December 2023 (open access: https://www.academia.edu/110124056/Young_Fairy_Census_2_2017_2023_)

Chapter 8

Sources

Magliocco, Sabina. 'The taming of the fae: Literary and folkloric fairies in modern paganisms', in Shai Feraro and Ethan Doyle White (eds), *Magic and Witchery in the Modern West: Celebrating the Twentieth Anniversary of 'The Triumph of the Moon'*, Palgrave Macmillan, London, 2019, 107–30

ILLUSTRATIONS AND MAPS

1. The ruins of the farmhouse near Goðafoss Waterfall, 2019. © Matthias Egeler. — 2
2. A manuscript page from an eighteenth-century copy of the Snorra Edda, ÍB 299 4to, 58r. The National and University Library of Iceland. — 21
3. The Bay of Naustvík, 2021. © Matthias Egeler. — 38
4. The elf church at Kirkjuklettur. © Matthias Egeler. — 38
5. The Neolithic grave mound of Newgrange in the valley of the Boyne. Tjp finn / CC BY-SA 4.0. — 45
6. The Cave of Crúachan. legendimages / Alamy. — 50
7. Lady Isabella Augusta Gregory. George Grantham Bain Collection, Library of Congress, LC-USZ62-104093. — 57
8. 'The Witch-Burning Case at Clonmel', *The Daily Graphic*, 1895. From the British Library archive / Bridgeman Images. — 64
9. The title page of Edmund Spenser, *The Faerie Queene*, 1596. Folger Shakespeare Library. — 91
10. The title page of King James I, *Daemonologie*, 1603. Wellcome Collection, CC BY 4.0. — 101
11. The Minister's Tree at Doon Hill, Aberfoyle, Scotland. Ann Stewart / Alamy. — 108
12. 'Infant Joy', plate 28 in William Blake, *Songs of Innocence and of Experience*, 1789. Yale Center for British Art, Paul Mellon Collection, B1978.43.1561. — 118
13. A grotesque fairy, detail from Henry Fuseli, *Titania, Bottom and the Fairies*, 1793/94. Historic Images / Alamy. — 120

14. Two winged fairies, illustration from Thomas Crofton Croker,   125
    Fairy Legends and Traditions of the South of Ireland, vol. 3,
    1828, p. 155.
15. John Anster Fitzgerald, *Fairy Hordes Attacking a Bat*, undated.   128
16. Richard Doyle, 'Triumphal March of the Elf-King', colour   130
    plate from *In Fairy Land: A Series of Pictures from the
    Elf-World by Richard Doyle. With a Poem by William
    Allingham*, 1870. The Miriam and Ira D. Wallach Division
    of Art, Prints and Photographs: Picture Collection,
    The New York Public Library Digital Collections.
17. A detail from Richard Dadd, *The Fairy Feller's Master-Stroke*,   132
    1855–64 (presented by Siegfried Sassoon in memory of
    his friend and fellow officer Julian Dadd, a great-nephew
    of the artist, and of his two brothers who gave their lives
    in the First World War, 1963). Tate.
18. The 'Luck of Edenhall', glass beaker decorated in enamel,   137
    fourteenth century. © Victoria and Albert Museum,
    London.
19. John Duncan, *The Riders of the Sidhe*, 1911.   139
    Artepics / Alamy.
20. Charles Buchel, poster advertising *Peter Pan*, 1904.   144
    © Victoria and Albert Museum, London.
21. Cast members in *Peter Pan*, Duke of York's Theatre,   146
    December 1907. © Victoria and Albert Museum, London.
22. 'Frances and the Fairies', the first of the Cottingley fairy   154
    photographs, 1917. GRANGER – Historical Picture
    Archive / Alamy.
23. 'Frances and the Leaping Fairy', August 1920.   157
    GRANGER – Historical Picture Archive / Alamy.
24. 'The Speedwell Fairy', from Cicely Mary Barker, *Flower*   164
    Fairies of the Spring, 1923. Charles Walker Collection /
    Alamy.
25. Elf houses in Hellisgerði Municipal Park, Hafnarfjörður.   197
    © Matthias Egeler.

Map 1.   The supernatural landscape surrounding the farm of   36
          Naustvík.
Map 2.   The supernatural countryside around Kilcurry, County   67
          Louth, in 1899. After Bryan J. Jones and W.B. Yeats,
          'Traditions and superstitions collected at Kilcurry, County
          Louth, Ireland', *Folklore*, x (1899), facing p. 119.

INDEX

Notes: page numbers in italics refer to illustrations. Icelandic names are entered by the forename followed by the patronymic, for example, 'Snorri Sturluson' not 'Sturluson, Snorri'.

abduction by fairies 107, 135
    Ireland 56, 68, 140–1
    in *Peter Pan* 151–2
    in Scottish ballads 84–7, 88
    see also changelings
Aberfoyle, Scotland 106, *108*
áes síde ('people of the fairy mounds') 43, 46, 47, 49, 54
Æsir (Old Norse gods) 16
álagablettur ('place of enchantment') 28–31, *36*, 37, *38*, 39
álfr (pl. *álfar*) ('elf' in Old Norse) 14–22, 23, 192, 195, 201
Allingham, William 129
Alp and *Alptraum* ('nightmare') 15, 134
alternative religions 206–8
Alvíssmál (*The Sayings of All-Wise*) 16, 174

angels 22, 100
animals *see* butterflies and fairies; horses; livestock
apples 47, 75, 76, 80, 81, 85
Arthur and Knights of the Round Table 6–7, 74–84, 92–3, 113, 139, 174
    Avalon as otherworld 74–5, 78, 88, 95, 202
    Island of Apples 75, 76, 78, 81
artists of elves and fairies 7, 90
    appearance of wings 116–19, *117*, 124, *125*
    Celtic Revival 138–9, *139*
    fairy painting 126–33, 141, 169, 203
    flower fairy books 162–3, *164*
    and Shakespeare 99
Ásdís Aðalbjörg Arnalds 194
Auðr *djúpauðga* (Audr the Deep-Minded) 42

Austrfararvísur (*Strophes on the Journey to the East*) 18–19
Avalon, Isle of 74–5, 78, 88, 95, 202

Ballad of Tam Lin 84, 86–8, 105, 121, 178, 202
  Janet 86–7, 88
  Margaret, Lady 86–7, 88
  Tam Lin 84, 86–7, 88, 105, 121, 178, 202
Barker, Cicely Mary 196, 197–8
  Flower Fairies of the Spring 162–3, *164*
Barrie, J.M. 144–52, 170, 203
  The Little White Bird 145
  Peter Pan and Wendy 145
  Peter Pan in Kensington Gardens 145, 147–8, 149, 150–2
  Peter Pan, or The Boy Who Would Not Grow Up 143, 144–7, *144*, *146*, 148–50, 162
Bible 99, 106, 109
Blake, William 116–17, 124, 127, 203
  Oberon, Titania and Puck with Fairies Dancing 117
  Songs of Innocence and of Experience 117, *118*
Bledsoe, Alex, *Tufa Novels* 132
blómálfar ('flower elves and fairies') 3, 14, 195–6, 197–8, 205–6, 208
Bodmer, Johann Jakob 133
Book of British Ballads, The 136
Book of Settlements 41, 42
Bottle-Back (name of Icelandic ghost) 39
Bradley, Marion Zimmer, *The Mists of Avalon* 207
Bran's Sea Voyage see *Immram Brain* (*Bran's Sea Voyage*)
Brentano, Clemens 120
Breton *lais* 78–9, 83, 84, 134, 176–7, 202

'Brewery of Eggshells' 65–6, 122
Britten, Benjamin 98
Brooks, Terry, *Shannara* series 178
Brothers Grimm see Grimm, Jacob and Wilhelm
brownies 109, 184, 207–8
Bull, Emma, *War for the Oaks* 181–2
butterflies and fairies 159, 192

Cave of Crúachan 49–50, *50*, 51
Celtic culture 33–4, 41–69, 75–81, 138
  see also Breton *lais*; Gaelic languages and culture; Ireland; Scotland
changelings 93, 152
  Iceland 32–4, 207
  Ireland 33–4, 56–69, 180–1, 202, 207
  A Midsummer Night's Dream 94–5
  protections against 33–4, 59–60, 107
children
  abuse and superstition 61–2
  flower fairies as 163, *164*
  and *Peter Pan* 147–52
  see also changelings
Christianity
  Iceland 1, 2, 18, 22, 23, 25, 33–4, 37, *38*, 39
  Kirk and popular beliefs 106–10
  and poor in Ireland 180–1
  Virgin Mary and fairies 83, 85
  and witch trials 99–106, 109
Cinderella (fairytale) 207
Cinderella (film) 207
Clarke, Susanna, *Jonathan Strange & Mr Norrell* 206
Cleary, Bridget 62–4, *64*
Codex Regius 15–16
Colfer, Eoin, *Artemis Fowl* 186–8
Collodi, Carlo, *Pinocchio* 207
Colquhoun, Ithell 167
Conan Doyle, Sir Arthur see Doyle, Sir Arthur Conan

INDEX

Concerning the Seizure of the Fairy Mound 44–6
Connle's Journey to the Otherworld 46–7, 76, 81, 176
Cottingley fairy photographs 7, 143, 152–62, *154*, *157*, 193–4, 195, 203–4, 205
courtly contexts 8–9, 73–89, 90, 92–3, 98, 113, 138–9, 202
    fantasy novels 178–9, 181–2
cows *see* livestock
Craufurd, Captain Quentin Charles Alexander 166–7
Croker, Thomas Crofton, *Fairy Legends and Traditions of the South of Ireland* 65, 122–3, 124, *125*
Crúachan, Ireland 49–50, *50*, 51
cruelty of fairies *128*, 129–31, 141, 146, 169, 182

Dadd, Richard 131–2
    Bethlem Royal Hospital, London 131
    The Fairy Feller's Master-Stroke 131, *132*
Dagda, the (king of Túatha Dé Dannan) 44–5, 47
daoine maithe see Good People
dark-elves (*døkkálfar*) 20–1, 22, 175
Darwin, Charles 126
De Gabáil in t-Sída (*Concerning the Seizure of the Fairy Mound*) 44–6
de Lint, Charles, *The Wild Wood* 185–6, *187*
death 58, 59–60, 62, 148, 149, 202
Denmark 134
Devil/Satan 85, 87, 105
    and witch trials 99–102, 104, 105, 202
Disney, Walt 145–6, 152, 167, 207
Domrémy, France 82–3, 88

Dowding, Hugh, Air Chief Marshal 167
Doyle, Sir Arthur Conan 129, 152–3, 155–6, 161
    The Coming of the Fairies 156, 158–9, 162, 165–6, 169, 170
Doyle, Charles Altamont 129, 155
Doyle, Richard 129–31, 155, 169
    In Fairy Land 129–31, *130*, 133
Duncan, John, *The Riders of the Sidhe* 138–9, *139*
Dunsany, Lord, *The King of Elfland's Daughter* 162
dwarves 16, 17, 192

Echtra Nerai (*Nera's Journey to the Otherworld*) 48–51, 52, 55
Echtrae Chonnlai (*Connle's Journey to the Otherworld*/*Connle's Adventure*) 46–7, 76, 81, 176
'eco-paganism' 188
Edenhall, Cumberland 135–6
Einar Ólafur Sveinsson 39
Elder Edda *see* Poetic (Elder) Edda
'elf' as term 4–5, 9, 133–4
'elf mound' (*síd*) 44–6, 47, 49, 50–1, 54, 208
Elfenbeauftragte ('Elves' Representative') 13, 189–90, 205
Elfland 85, 86, 87
    queen of 85, 177, 178
Elizabeth I, Queen of England 92, 93, 97, 99
Ellis, Ivy Anne 164
Elucidarius (Latin text) 22, 23
Elwood, A.J. (Alison Littlewood), *The Cottingley Cuckoo* 161–2
Erl-King (German literature) 134–5
    see also fairy king

Erla Stefánsdóttir 8, 13, 14,
    189–94, 195, 196–7, 198,
    205, 208
    Lífssýn mín 191, 193
    Örsögur 191–2

Fairy Investigation Society 144,
    165–71, 204
fairy kings 84, 105, 130, *130*,
    134–6
    see also Dagda, the; Erl-King;
    Oberon
'fairy mounds'
    in Ireland 44–6, 47, 49, 50–1,
    54, 208
    in Scotland 107, 149
fairy painting 126–33, 141, 169,
    203
    see also Barker, Cicely Mary
fairy queens 92–3, 102, 104
    in fantasy novels 178–9, 182
    in Scottish ballads 84–7, 88,
    177, 178, 202
    see also Mab, Queen; Titania
Fairy Tale: A True Story (film) 161
fantasy novels 165, 177–88
farming 45, 187
    Iceland 2, 24–5, 28–31, 32,
    34–40, 201
    see also livestock
Fata Morgana 207
fée ('fairy') 4, 9
Findhorn community, Scotland
    187
Fitzgerald, John Anster 127–9,
    169
    The Artist's Dream 127
    Fairy Hordes Attacking a Bat
    128–9, *128*
    The Nightmare 127
flower fairies 7–8, 169–70, 203–4
    Barker's books 162–3, *164*,
    196, 197–8
    Erla Stefándóttir's writings
    192–3
    'flower elves' (*blómálfar*) 3, 14,
    195–6, 197–8, 205–6, 208

in *Peter Pan in Kensington
    Gardens* 150–1
Tolkien's dismissal of 173–4
folklore research 7, 119–23, 203
    Fairy Investigation Society 144,
    165–71, 204
    Grimm Brothers 23, 119–22,
    137, 203
    in Iceland 14, 23–4, 123
    Irish Folklore Commission
    54–5
    and Irish national identity
    138–42
    Kirk's *The Secret
    Commonwealth* 106–10,
    113, 122, 149, 184
food and drink 85, 127
    abducted humans 61, 68
    apples 75, 76, 80, 81, 85
    and elf mounds 45–6, 47, 54
    fairy banquets 104–5, 136
    Lai de Guingamor 80, 81
forests as settings 76–7, 79, 80,
    94, 175, 176–7, 178–9,
    202
France 76–83, 96
    Breton *lais* 78–9, 83, 84, 134,
    176–7, 202
    Joan of Arc 81–3, 88
    Lai de Lanval 76–8, 80, 88,
    175
Fuseli, Henry 116, 124, 127, 203
    Titania, Bottom and the Fairies
    119, *120*

Gaelic languages and culture 9,
    52, 106, 139
    links to Iceland 6, 8, 33–4,
    41–3, 65–6, 205
    see also Ireland; Scotland
Gandálfr ('elf who can do magic')
    16–17
Gardner, Edward L. 154–6, 158,
    159–61, 167, 193, 195,
    205
Gardner, Gerald B., *Witchcraft
    Today* 207

INDEX

Gaynor, Hazel, *The Cottingley Secret* 161
Geoffrey of Monmouth 74, 75
Germanic languages 4–5, 9, 10, 15, 133–4
Germany 4–5, 119–22, 133–7
   Elfenbeauftragte 13, 189–90, 205
Gesta Danorum (Denmark) 51–2
Goðafoss Waterfall 1, 2–3, 29–30
gods 1, 2, 15–16, 18–19, 19, 142
Goethe, J.W. von, *Erlkönig* 134–5
Good Fairy 207
Good People (*daoine maithe*) 55, 56–69, 139
Goodfellow, Robin (Puck) 95, 96
Gowdie, Isobel 104–5
Gregory, Isabella Augusta, Lady 56, *57*, 58, 60, 61, 138–40, 143, 162
   Gods and Fighting Men 138, 142
   Visions and Beliefs in the West of Ireland 139
Griffiths, Annie 153, 154
Griffiths, Frances 153–4, *154*, 156, *157*, 161, 162
Grimm, Jacob and Wilhelm 4–5, 123
   folktale collections 23, 119–22, 137, 203
   Irische Elfenmärchen 65, 122, 124
Grímnismál (*The Sayings of Grímnir*) 16
Guinevere, Queen 77–8
Guingamor 79–81, 82–3, 88, 175
Gunnell, Terry 194

Hadingus, King 51–2
Hall, S.C. (Anna Maria Hall) 136
Heine, Heinrich 137
Hellisgerði Municipal Park, Reykjavík 196–7, *197*
Hennen, Bernhard, *Drachenelfen* 178

Her Oluf hand rider saa vide (Danish ballad) 134
Herder, J.G., *Erlkönigs Tochter* 134
Hidden People (*huldufólk*)
   in *álagablettur* 28–31, *36*, 37, *38*, 39, 208
   and changelings 32–4, 65, 207
   Christian faith 25, 33, 37, *38*, 39
   differences to 'Reykjavík fairies' 26, 40, 195, 196
   homes and human neighbours 25–6, 31, 34, 37, 39, 42–3
   mirroring human life and activity 24–7, 34–40, 201–2
   in rural Iceland 1–3, 24–40, 89, 123, 192, 193, 194
Hohlbein, Wolfgang, *Chroniken der Elfen* 178
Horne, Janet 106
horses 29, 56, 63, 78, 85, 87, 178
house elf 183–4
   Dobby (*Harry Potter* series) 183–4
   see also brownies
huldufólk see Hidden People
Huldufólksbrekka, Iceland 28–9
Huon de Bordeaux (romance) 96

Iceland 13–40, 172–3
   2006/7 survey of folk beliefs 194–5
   álagablettur 28–9, *36*, 37, *38*, 39
   conversion to Christianity 1, 2, 18
   Elfenbeauftragte ('Elves' Representative') 13, 189–90, 205
   elves' response to humans on land 1–2, *2*, 3, 18, 28–30
   empty spaces and need for company 39–40, 209
   'flower elves' (*blómálfar*) 3, 14, 195–6, 197–8, 205–6, 208
   Gaelic influences 6, 8, 33–4, 41–3, 65–6, 201, 205

Goðafoss Waterfall 1–3, 29–30
medieval Iceland 13–14,
    14–22, 89, 174–5, 208
modern folktales from rural
    areas 14, 23–40, 113, 123,
    194
present-day elves in urban areas
    13, 14, 26, 40, 173,
    188–98, 204–6, 208
settlers from Ireland and
    Scandinavia 41–2
terms for elves and fairies 9,
    14–15, 24
see also álfr (pl. álfar); Hidden
    People; Reykjavík
illness
  healing by magic 103
  and superstition 58–60, 62–4,
    180–1
  see also poverty and illness
Immram Brain (Bran's Sea Voyage)
    47–8, 76, 81, 175, 176
Ireland 41–69, 113, 175, 207–8,
    209
  abduction and changelings
    33–4, 56–69, 140–1,
    180–1, 202, 207
  and Celtic culture 81
  elite medieval literature 43–53,
    54, 76, 78, 81, 138–9,
    141–2, 174, 202
  Gaelic influences in Iceland 6,
    8, 33–4, 41–3, 65–6, 201,
    205
  Good People and rural folktales
    55, 56–69, 122, 139
  language and terminology for
    fairies 9, 55
  national identity and folktales
    137–42
  oral tradition and rural beliefs
    54–5, 139, 201–2
Irish Folklore Commission
    54–5

James I, King of England (VI of
    Scotland) 99–106

Daemonologie 100, *101*, 102,
    103, 105, 109, 202
Januals ljóð (Old Norse) 78
Joan of Arc 81–3, 88
Johnson, Marjorie Thelma
    167–71
Jón Árnason 24
  Icelandic Legends and Fairytales
    123

Kent, Hannah, *The Good People*
    179–81
Kilcurry, Ireland 66, *67*, 68
kings see fairy kings
Kipling, Rudyard, *Puck of Pook's
    Hill* 125
Kirk, Robert (the 'Fairy Minister')
    92, 106–10, 133
  The Secret Commonwealth 107,
    109–10, 113, 122, 149,
    184
Kushner, Ellen, *Thomas the
    Rhymer* 178–9

Lai de Graelent 78
Lai de Guingamor 79–81, 82–3,
    88, 175
Lai de Lanval 76–8, 80, 88,
    175
Landnámabók (*Book of
    Settlements*) 41, 42
Lang, Andrew 174
Lanval (knight) 76–8, 80, 88,
    175
Laoidh Oisín ar Thír na nÓg (*The
    Lay of Oisín in the Land of
    the Young/Ageless*) 52–3, 56,
    81
Lay of Vǫlundr, The 17–18,
    174
Letcher, Andy 187–8
light-elves (*ljósálfar*) 20–1, 22,
    175
literature 7
  collections of folktales 119–23
  Conan Doyle's theories 156,
    158–9

INDEX

courtly and aristocratic sources and subjects 73–89, 90, 113, 178–9, 181–2, 202
fantasy novels in present day 165, 177–88
foreign influences in Germany 134–7
Ireland in Middle Ages 43–53, 54, 76, 78, 138–9, 141–2, 175–6, 202
Kirk's *The Secret Commonwealth* 106–10, 113, 122, 184
Old French literature 76–83, 84, 96, 134, 175, 176–7, 202
Old Norse literature 14–22
Peter Pan 143, 144–52, 162, 203
Tolkien's reworking of tradition 173–8
Tudor literature in England 92–9
winged fairies in eighteenth-century poetry 115, 203
writings in early 1900s 162–7
see also Arthur and Knights of Round Table
Littlewood, Alison *see* Elwood, A.J.
livestock 25, 29, 34–7, 105
Longfellow, Henry Wadsworth 136
love affairs and relationships 32, 98, 107, 178–9
Breton *lais* 76–8, 79–81, 80, 82, 88, 175
Ireland 46–7, 49–50, 51, 52–3
Scottish ballads 84–7, 88, 177, 202
Luck of Edenhall, The (ballad) 136
'Luck of Edenhall' (goblet) 136, *137*

Mab, Queen 97–8, 148, 149, 151
Mac Óc, the 44–5
Magliocco, Sabina 187
Maltman, Stein 103, 104
Marie de France 76–8, 80, 88, 175
Maurer, Konrad 33, 123
Mendelssohn, Felix 98
Merlin (Arthurian figure) 75
Milton, John, *Paradise Lost* 133
Mirrlees, Hope, *Lud-in-the-Mist* 162
Morgain la Fée/Morgen 75, 76, 78
Müller, Wolfgang 189
Musgrave family of Edenhall 135–6

nature
environmental issues 161, 165–6, 169, 185–8, 189–93, 204–5, 209
and Fairy Investigation Society 169–71, 204
flower fairy books 162–3, *164*
spirits 10, 160–1, 167, 169
theosophical views 159–61, 165–6, 205
see also apples; environmental issues; flower fairies; forests as settings
Naustvík farm, Iceland 34–7, *38*, 39
Nera's Journey to the Otherworld 48–51, 52, 55
Newgrange Neolithic mound 44–5, *45*
Niamh (mythical princess) 52–3
North Berwick witch trial 100

Ó hEochaidh, Seán 59, 61
Oberon 95–6, 98, 117, 131
Oisín (Irish warrior) 52–3, 56, 81
Old Norse literature 14–22, 174–5
oral tradition
Grimm Brothers 121–2
Iceland 14, 23–40, 113, 123, 194

Ireland 54–5, 122, 139
  scholarly collection 123, 124
  Scottish ballads 84–7, 88, 121, 178
Orff, Carl 98–9
otherworlds
  Avalon and Arthur 74–5, 78, 88, 95, 202
  food and drink 45–6, 47, 54, 61, 68, 80, 81, 85
  Irish literature 44–53, 60, 175–6
  A Midsummer Night's Dream 95, 98
  Scottish ballads 84–6, 88, 177, 178–9, 202
  time differences 48, 50, 51, 80, 81, 85, 175
  witch trials 104–5, 177
Ovid, *Metamorphoses* 96–7

Paracelsus (Theophrastus Bombastus von Hohenheim), *Liber de nymphis* 114–15, 117
Perrault, Charles, *Cinderella* 207
Peter Pan 143, 144–52, 162, 170, 203
Peter Pan (films) 145–6
Phillips, Sir Thomas 131
Photographing Fairies (film) 161
photography *see* Cottingley fairy photographs
Pinocchio in Italian tradition 207
Poetic (Elder) Edda 15–16, 17
Pole, Major Wellesley Tudor 167
Pope, Alexander, *The Rape of the Lock* 115
poverty and illness
  and courtly tales 88–9
  rural France 82–3, 88
  rural Iceland 26–7
  rural Ireland 58–60, 61, 89, 139, 140–1, 180–1
Pratchett, Terry
  Discworld novels 182–3
  The Wee Free Men 132

Prose Edda *see* Snorra (Prose) Edda
Puck 95, 96, 98, 99, 117
Purcell, Henry, *The Fairy-Queen* 98
Purkiss, Diane 5, 84

queens *see* fairy queens; Guinevere, Queen

Ragna Benedikta Garðarsdóttir 194
religions 206–7, 208
  see also Christianity
Reykjavík, Iceland 13, 14, 26, 40, 173, 189–98, 206, 208
roads 27–8, 188, 189–91
  fairy roads 66, 67, 68
Roche, Anne (Nance) 180
Romanticism 116–19, 121, 125
Rowling, J.K.
  The Casual Vacancy 184–5
  Harry Potter series 183–4
rural contexts 7, 8, 9, 88–9, 90
  Iceland 13–40, 89, 113, 123, 194, 201, 208
  Ireland 54–5, 56–69, 89, 113, 139, 140–1, 201–2

Sapkowski, Andrzej, *The Witcher* series 178
Saxo Grammaticus, *Gesta Danorum* 51–2
Sayings of All-Wise, The 16, 174
Sayings of Grímnir, The 16
Schubert, Franz 135
Scotland 6, 43, 99–110, 181–2, 207–8
  ballads 84–7, 88, 121, 177, 178–9, 202
  Scandinavian colonies in 41–2
  see also Kirk, Robert; witch trials
Scott, Sir Walter 107, 121, 135–6
Seelie and Unseelie Courts 181–2
Shakespeare, William 90, 202–3

A Midsummer Night's Dream 4, 7, 93–9, 105–6, 113, 117, 133, 134, 183, 202, 208
Queen Mab in *Romeo and Juliet* 97–8, 202
síd see 'elf mound' (*síd*)
Sigvatr Þórðarson 18–19
Sir Landevale (Launfal/ Lambewell) 78
size of fairies
  Blake's poems and art 117
  Conan Doyle and theosophy 159–60, 162, 174, 204
  fairy painting 128, 129, 131
  Fuseli's work 119
  human size 26, 203
  reduction in size and power 203–4, 208
  Shakespeare 98, 208
Sleigh, Bernard 163–7
  An Ancient Mappe of Fairyland 163–4
  'Faery Calendar' (with Ellis) 164
  The Gates of Horn 164–7, 169, 181, 185
Snorra (Prose) Edda 20–2, *21*, 175
Snorri Sturluson 20, 23, 25, 175
social contexts
  and developments in art and literature 163
  elite medieval Icelandic writings 22–3, 24
  elite medieval Irish writings 54, 138, 141–2, 202
  and elves in Iceland 24
  and Fairy Investigation Society 167, 169–70
  Irish accounts of popular beliefs 107
  Kirk's recording of popular beliefs 107, 109–10, 113, 122, 149
  persecution of popular beliefs 90

poverty and illness in rural Ireland 58–60, 61, 89, 139, 140–1, 180–1
scholarly collections and wider distribution 123, 124
see also courtly contexts
Spenser, Edmund, *The Faerie Queene* 90, *91*, 92–3, 95, 97, 113
spiritualism 155, 166–7, 204
Stothard, Thomas 116
sylphs as spirits of air 115
Szilagyi, Steve, *Photographing Fairies* 161

Tam Lin *see Ballad of Tam Lin*
Theosophical Society 154–5, 193, 198
theosophy 154–5, 158, 159–61, 167, 174, 195, 203–4
  Iceland 190, 193–4, 205
  and Yeats's views 141
Thomas of Erceldoune (poem) 84–6, 88, 95, 105, 121, 177, 178–9, 202
Thomas the Rhymer (Thomas of Erceldoune) 84–6, 88, 105, 121, 177, 178–9, 202
Tieck, Ludwig, *The Elves* 136–7
time in otherworld 80, 81, 85, 175
  fairy mounds 48, 50, 51, 175
Tinker Bell 145–6, 149, 152, 170, 203
Tír na nÓg (Land of Youth) 52–3
Titania 95, 96–7, 98, 117, 119, 131
Tolkien, J.R.R. 8, 9, 172, 173–8
  The Hobbit 173, 175, 177
  The Lord of the Rings 16–17, 173, 175–7
  'On Fairy-stories' 173–4
  The Silmarillion 175
trolls in Iceland 39
Túatha Dé (tribes of the gods) 43, 44–6

Túatha Dé Danann (tribes of the goddess Danu) 43, 138–9, 141–2

Uhland, Ludwig, *Das Glück von Edenhall* 135–6
umskiptingar (changelings) 32–4, 65, 207
Unnur Diljá Teitsdóttir 194
urban contexts 8–9, 113–42, 203, 207
   fantasy novels 181–8
   present-day Iceland 13, 14, 26, 40, 173, 188–98, 204–6, 208–9
   Sleigh's cases 165
   see also Peter Pan

Vanir (Old Norse gods) 16
Virgin Mary and fairy figures 83, 85
Vǫlundarkviða (*The Lay of Vǫlundr*) 17–18, 174

Wagner, Richard, *Die Feen* 137
Wales, fairy narratives 207
Warner, Sylvia Townsend, *Kingdoms of Elfin* 206
water and folklore 55, 82–3
Wicca movement 207
Wieland, Christoph Martin 134
winged fairies 172
   emergence in art and literature 7, 114–19, *117*, 124, *125*
   in Erla Stefánsdóttir's writings 192, 193
   in fairy painting 126–33, 203
   sightings in early twentieth century 168–9
   theosophy view 159–60, 174, 204
   Tinker Bell in *Peter Pan* 146
   Tolkien's dismissal 173–4
   see also angels
witch trials
   Joan of Arc 81–3, 88
   Scotland 7, 90, 99–106, 109, 177, 202–3
witches
   fear of sorceresses in medieval tales 176–7
   in Terry Pratchett's novels 183
woods *see* forests as settings
Wright, Arthur 153
Wright, Elsie 153–4, 156, 161, 162
Wright, Polly 153, 154

Yeats, William Butler 138, 139–42, 143, 162
   Fairy and Folk Tales 140
   Irish Fairy Tales 140
   'The Stolen Child' 140–1
Young, Simon 166, 168

Zophanías Pétursson 190